SWIMMING
AGAINST
THE STREAM

Christmas — my love

TIM WATERSTONE

[handwritten signature]

[handwritten] 2006

SWIMMING

AGAINST

THE STREAM

LAUNCHING YOUR BUSINESS

AND MAKING YOUR LIFE

MACMILLAN

First published 2006 by Macmillan
an imprint of Pan Macmillan Ltd
Pan Macmillan, 20 New Wharf Road, London N1 9RR
Basingstoke and Oxford
Associated companies throughout the world
www.panmacmillan.com

ISBN-13: 978-1-4050-5525-3
ISBN-10: 1-4050-5525-1

9 8 7 6 5 4 3 2 1

A CIP catalogue record for this book is available from
the British Library.

Typeset by Intype Libra, London
Printed and bound in Great Britain by
Mackays of Chatham plc, Chatham, Kent

FOR CHRISTOPHER THOMSON

Contents

One

TRUST IN YOUR COURAGE

If you can make one heap of all your winnings
And risk it all on one turn of pitch-and-toss,
And lose, and start again at your beginnings
And never breathe a word about your loss; . . .
Yours is the Earth and everything that's in it,
And – which is more – you'll be a Man, my son!

Rudyard Kipling, 'If'

No one reads Kipling today, and they are the poorer for it, but everyone is familiar with those other great lines from 'If' that are inscribed above the door of the players' changing rooms at Wimbledon; that lovely juxtaposition of meeting with Triumph and Disaster, and treating those two impostors just the same.

What Kipling encapsulated in 'If' was the entrepreneurial life. Having the courage to put all your winnings back on the table and start again, meeting great triumphs and great disasters in the same way; risking everything, saving your breath on self-pity; dreaming great dreams.

That is what wins – extreme courage, real self-knowledge, and a certain simplicity and straightforwardness of mind. If you have it within you to add one extra dimension – a passion, linked to a sense of rightness, an instinct for what really matters, a contempt for duplicity and deception – then you'll be, as Kipling puts it, a man.

'I think I overcame every single one of my personal shortcomings by the sheer passion I brought to my work', claimed Sam Walton, the folksy founder of Wal-Mart, a company these days so huge and so powerful that it moves the economies of entire countries, but forty years ago was no more than a small town American general store. 'I do not know if you are born with this kind of passion, or if you can learn it. But I do know you need it,' he went on to say. And of course he is right.

You absolutely do need sheer passion and raw commitment if your entrepreneurial dream, your start-up, is to succeed. As many as ninety-five out of one hundred start-ups (and I do not mean dotcoms) will fail every year, in the US and in the UK, so – yes – boy, do you need it. But, like Sam Walton, I wonder if you can learn this kind of passion or whether you have to be born with it. I think probably the latter. It goes with the ability to shrug at risk and survive stress.

It is indeed sheer passion that gives great entrepreneurial ventures their sheen and their electricity. And to some extent Walton is right in his additional claim: the driving, blind passion of the best of the entrepreneurial leaders does act within their working lives to help to camouflage, even to overwhelm and overcome, other facets of their characters that are less helpful to the cause.

Over the course of this book we will sometimes look at Walton's ideas about thrift, industry and the square deal – the famous 'Sam's Ten Rules for Building a Business'. They may seem pure Ben Franklin, but they certainly worked for Wal-Mart, which is now, overwhelmingly, the largest retailer in the world with a hundred million customers a week, and another branch opening somewhere in the world every three days. And we will doff our caps to Sam. 'Swim against the stream' is his dictum, and there is a resonance in the phrase that captures precisely the cussed independence of spirit of the true entrepreneur. 'Go the other way,' he says. 'Ignore the conventional wisdom. If everybody is doing it one way, there is a good chance that you can find your niche by going in exactly the opposite direction. But be prepared for a lot of folks to wave you down and tell you that you are headed the wrong way.'

Passion, then, and independence of mind are what Sam Walton preaches. But it is the vision that comes first, and all else flows from that. All the great consumer businesses have been built from a picture born and carried in the founder's head; right from the very start a finished, defined picture of what the offer is to be, who it is to be aimed at and why it is that it will win. And that is the point – winning. And 'winning' for the founding entrepreneur is not so much making a fortune as making the point, defeating the sceptics, acting as a catalyst for change. It's the public projection of a personal vision, and a personal passion to succeed with it.

My own logic behind Waterstone's, when, with just £6,000 of my own left in my pocket, I founded the business in 1982, lay in the fact that as a devoted reader I found it inexplicable that a city as great and culturally diverse as London had within it barely a single stockholding literary bookshop, and certainly not one that was open past noon on Saturdays, let alone in the weekday evenings. New York had great bookshops open at every hour, and Paris too. Rome also. San Francisco. Boston. All the civilized world over. So why not London?

It was intuition of course on my part, and intuition only. What else could it be? The business schools teach that the four hallmarks of good new business launches are these: sound market research, skilful planning, a strong customer focus and a diligent execution performed in line with the plan. Well – I'll tell you what I think. It is difficult to argue with an orthodoxy of that sort at first glance – and yet a reliance on these classic maxims is not in the least how an entrepreneur actually operates. It certainly was not how I was thinking at that moment. And the fact that I was not gave me one of my points of advantage against the overwhelming market leader of the time, WHSmith.

It is always so. The big corporations' simple, blind, safety-first reliance on these classic maxims is invariably a severe mistake. It disadvantages them against the entrepreneur. For what is the weak link in it all? Market research. It always is. In existing markets intelligent researchers can forecast demand and evaluate competitive situations quite accurately. But when markets for any new products emerge (in particular for new technologies, but actually for any innovation or unorthodoxy), the only thing you can depend on is that all the research will be wrong. Even research from the best and the brightest, such as Proctor & Gamble, which we will discuss later.

It is not market research, but intuition that is the only way through. It is intuition that is crucial if a corporation is to enjoy continued growth into the future, find new markets, and exploit them. Intuition, and nothing else, will have to find those markets. But big corporations do not do intuition. What they do is safety. It is the reverse for entrepreneurs, who are all intuition and have contempt for safety. Big corporations will compare the new technology or product with the established technology and product, and then decide that the new is unproven and risky and the established proven and risk-free. You could say that corporations will – quite without fail – give the right answers to the wrong questions. It is not true, for example, to say that too many new, innovative products fail because the market research around them is faulty. The market research would not have been faulty, but irrelevant, and would have served only to confuse.

So, at Waterstone's we used not one jot of market research in deciding our action plan. We just did it. And in that I would guess that we were typical of most, if not all, successful entrepreneurial start-ups. These arise almost every time from a founder's probably sudden, blinding epiphany of vision for a market breakthrough in an area in which he or she has expertise. We could not afford market research. But what market research could have helped us anyway? The fact was that the bookshops of the sort we were looking for were not there. We knew with total clarity what we wanted them to be, and we knew they would work. Therefore we would open them ourselves: 'Waterstone's' (I still recall the rush of intense pleasure as I saw the name go up over the door of our very first store, in London's Old Brompton Road). My dream, the picture in my head, my bottom-of-the-barrel £6,000, my cry for literature, my personal statement, my name, the public encapsulation of my own personality. My bookshops. 'Waterstone's.'

Waterstone's would be better than any bookshops any-where. 'Better', for me, meant reliable, comprehensive, expertly chosen stock, so we decided to present an offer of such depth and range that in investment terms we had literally twice the stock-per-square-foot cover to that of other booksellers in Britain. It meant nice big stores, with a genuinely literary atmosphere, in residentially convenient locations. It meant opening as extensively as we could, including Sundays. (In those days opening on Sunday was ille-gal, but we thought the law an ass and we did it – running a public campaign on this issue, protesting that bookshops offered urban communities an unmatched cultural and leisure amenity on Sunday afternoons.) And it meant arts graduates, and only arts graduates, confidently literary people, staffing and running those stores. They would be unfettered by any excess of central control. All recruits would be hand-picked (by me personally, always) for their book knowledge and enthusiasm to use that knowledge. We told our people to regard their bookshops not so much as stores within a national chain, but as independent bookshops which just happened to carry the Waterstone's name. Independent book-shops of the very highest quality. And we told them to accept personal responsibility for the achievement of that.

They did so. And in doing that, as Andrew Stilwell, one

of Waterstone's earliest staff members, reminisced in 2004 in the *Guardian*, they accepted that

> managers, as part of their autonomy, were also encouraged to become good business people, rigorously mindful of profit and loss, balance sheets, business plans, budgets and forecasts – with the result that some of the most successful independent bookshops are now being run by former friends and colleagues from Waterstone's . . . We strove to achieve the key skill of a good bookseller and the source of his/her pride in the job; not just intelligently stocking what people will expect to find in a bookshop, but second-guessing what customers will be surprised and excited by.

That was Waterstone's and the vision. Hardly rocket science, and the better for that. Passionate book people running individual, passionately committed bookshops, and, free of centralism, taking personal responsibility for the quality of their bookshops and their financial results. We rolled out the stores across the country straightaway rather than concentrating only in the London area, as we had originally planned. And we did that because we became convinced that, outside a few travel books, reading tastes are universal rather than local. We barely changed our offer at all, region by region. We believed it would succeed anywhere. And we backed our hunch, opening, for example, a few years down the line in Gateshead in the north-east of England, an industrial town with raging unemployment and very low rates of higher education – probably the least promising social demographics you could find for literary bookselling anywhere in the country. We gave Gateshead our absolutely standard literary offer, exactly as we would in Cambridge or Oxford. It worked just fine. Never mind the demographics. Expose people to books, possibly for effectively the first time in their lives, and they will find within themselves an interest and a cultural capacity they perhaps never thought they had.

So, no market research for us as we set out on our way. If we had commissioned market research, it would no doubt have confirmed what everyone was telling us – that the death of the book was imminent. Everyone – the trade, the financial community, the general public – had been brainwashed by media futurology to believe that. The future was to be high tech and only high tech, and the very idea of the printed word on paper would prove in time to be an anachronism. City bankers – I remember them individually, I met them, I tried and failed to raise money from them – were scornful. They pronounced that it was not just the book that would shortly be dead, but newspapers too. No one would read anything by the time the end of the twentieth century came along, except for factual material in electronic form. Television would sweep the book away. And, incidentally, sweep away cinemas as well. Who on earth would go to inconvenient, draughty cinemas when you could watch movies on television in the comfort of your home?

The book was dead in the water, the movie-in-the-cinema was dead in the water. That was what the marketing futurologists were saying, and with absolute conviction. Rather as in future years they would tell us, with similar conviction, that there would never be a general consumer market for mobile telephones, as people would find the wretched things too much of a nuisance to carry around . . .

But what happened? Well – what happened in the mobile telephone market was Nokia, an outstanding example of a company that had the courage to drop business units of low or slow potential and concentrate entirely on one that they had the intuition to believe would prove to be a sensation. I repeat – they did it by intuition. The market research around the subject gave them no lead at all. It all sounds easy, given what we know now, but Nokia's decision was very brave, way back in the late eighties, when the mobile telephone market was hardly off the ground. What Nokia understood was that they would have to get under the skins of the emerging consumers. They believed that the market, when it developed, was going to extend a country mile beyond the cold, business productivity tool that the contemporary researchers of the time thought was to be the mobile telephone's sole usage. They believed something quite different – that the market would in time actually stretch way into the limitless field of informal social interaction. Chat, putting it bluntly. Lifestyle. Entertainment. People across the world would become addicted users. Design would be important, Nokia guessed, so they found world-class designers. Fashion too, street cred, funkiness, so they made multicoloured devices. Nokia read it exactly right. Their reward is that they are now probably one of the half-dozen most recognized, and thus inherently valuable, brands in the world. They deserve it.

Let us say it again – Nokia, ignoring the opinion of others, ignoring research, just used their intuition. Their action underlined the point that hypothetical market research – 'what if' research – probing the consumer about products that do not yet exist, always, quite without fail, proves later to be nonsense. As George Bernard Shaw said, the British people never know what they want until they are given it. Research-based futurology never works. What happened to mobile phones was Nokia. What happened to books is that the market proved to grow at nearly 5 per cent per annum compound (at current prices) since Waterstone's was founded twenty-three years ago, and as much as 6 per cent compound since 1994. What happened to movies was the multiplex cinemas. Cinema-going by the end of the century was at the highest level in Britain since the 1920s.

Do the affairs of man necessarily improve? J. M. Keynes, writing in 1900:

> The inhabitant of London could order by telephone, sipping his morning tea in bed, the various products of the whole earth and reasonably expect their early delivery upon his doorstep; he could at the same moment and by the same means adventure his wealth in the natural resources and new enterprises of

any quarter of the world, and share, without exertion or even trouble, in their prospective fruits and advantages.

Futurology? One-click ordering may now have jazzy shopping trolley icons, but it is still home delivery. That is old, not new. E-mail may be a hundred times superior to snail mail, but Amazon still delivers your books by post or courier. Ordering your groceries from Ocado does not sound so far removed from ringing up the village store and getting them sent round in the van. And how wrong can the received wisdom of the time prove to be . . .

'Everything that can be invented, has been invented'
– **Charles Duell, US Commissioner for Patents, 1879.**

'I do not think that the wireless waves I have discovered will have any practical application' – **Heinrich Hertz, 1894.**

'It is apparent to me that the possibilities of the aeroplane have been exhausted' – **Thomas Edison, 1931.**

'There is not the slightest indication that energy will ever be obtainable from the atom' – **Albert Einstein.**

'There is a world market for six computers'
– **Thomas J. Watson, chairman of IBM, 1956.**

'There is no reason for any individual to have a computer in their home' – **John Olsen, president of Digital, 1977.**

No futurology for us at Waterstone's then, and no market research. Actually, that is wrong. There was some market research, but it was free and of incomparable quality. Site selection was largely a process of following in other people's footsteps. Marks & Spencer to be precise. The Marks & Spencer property specialists and their demographic models were good enough for us – where they opened, we opened. But we did so with one crucial difference. We could not take on prime rents, so what we did was open near to Marks & Spencer, but round the corner; off prime side streets some-times, preferably – and this was quite crucial – in buildings of architectural interest. We trusted in the theory that if our stores were good enough – more than merely good enough, wonderful enough – then within a period of just a few months the word would get out, and people would set out to find us. And when they had, we would get our sales per square foot that we aimed for, but at much more moderate ongoing rental cost (not just in the short term, but with increasing benefit throughout the whole tenure of the long leases we sought).

We opened near WHSmith too, but that was for a rather different reason. We liked to tease them – the mighty WHSmith, holders at that time of by far the most dominant market share in books – by opening our stores as close to them as possible and taking them straight on. Right beside them, if we could. And another one right across the street. If our appetite in those days for so aggressively pulling WHSmith's august tail surprises, I can only say in explana-tion that we had learnt that their directors were – publicly, and no doubt in their own eyes amusingly – at the time engaged in running a book, wagering on exactly which month we would go belly up. That joke must have palled for them a little when barely seven years after our start-up they asked us if they could invest in our business. We negotiated an entry price per share that represented a multiple of almost fifty-three times for the founders (527p against 10p). Their investment price had also had added to it a ceremonial one million pounds for the fact that they had fired me in 1981, an act from which the creation of Waterstone's flowed a few months later.

I talk of teasing WHSmith. Maybe I should be a little more honest, as 'teasing' is not quite right. There is nothing like a highly personalized enmity, edging into vindictiveness, to get the entrepreneurial juices flowing. It is all part of the mindset. 'We're at our best when we've got a particular enemy,' Charles Dunstone of Carphone Warehouse is quoted as saying. 'We're good haters.' Think Branson and British Airways. Dyson and Hoover. Gates and IBM. Particularly colourfully these days, and in an enmity that holds the City of London agog, Michael Spencer of Icap and Terry Smith of Collins Stewart. As for me, I used to dream, nightly, of the WHSmith directors and the circumstances of their firing me. 'I don't mind much what you do now,' the chairman had said to me as he walked out of the room, shrugging. He then looked back, briefly. 'Maybe we'd prefer it if you didn't open any bookshops.' What prescience. 'Eureka!' I thought. 'Bookshops!'

The first Waterstone's was opened the following September. In the interim, trying desperately to keep my £6,000 untouched, on one occasion I went to sign on for the dole at my local unemployment benefit office. I stood in line, and, just as my turn came up, I turned away and fled the building. I sat in the borrowed car outside, alone, and cried. I was bigger than this. I was not going to stand in line for the dole. I was not a loser. I had six children who looked up to me. Waterstone's was on its way. Waterstone's would win.

I was still dreaming about WHSmith and its chairman until 1997, fifteen years later, when, with my personal circumstances then rather different, I launched a personal hostile bid for the WHSmith group at 385p a share, backed by UBS Warburg. The bid failed in the end – just – but it was extremely good fun. Personal, rather than corporate, hostile bids are very rare. It had been unbelievably enjoyable. And it proved to be exactly what I needed to clear my system. No therapist could have invented such a cure. The dreams stopped, as if by magic, and have never returned.

'If you love your work, you will be out there every day trying to do it the best you possibly can, and pretty soon everybody around you will catch the passion from you – like a fever,' Sam Walton said.

I did love Waterstone's, and I very much still do, for Waterstone's made my life, and defined my life. We believed we had a winner – we knew we had a winner – and, at least for me personally, committing myself passionately and unswervingly to that win was as necessary to me, and as instinctive, as breathing itself. At our best I felt that we made at the time – as pioneers, first movers in our field – a unique contribution to the day-to-day cultural good health of the nation. Greater than anybody's. And that may well still be true today, however much more crowded the competitive environment may have become. Like Sam Walton, I was out there every day trying to do the best I possibly could. And others around me – they know who they are, and they know that I live for ever in their debt – did catch that passion from me, and ran with it.

It is like a fever. No doubt it happened to Gordon Self-ridge, creator of the brilliantly focused eponymous Oxford Street department store, targeted then so exquisitely and precisely at the suburban middle class and at lower-middle-class London. It happened with Terence Conran in the 1950s, with his finely conceived, skilfully presented Habitat stores. It happened to Selim Zilka in the 1960s, as his Mothercare start-up – just a dream in his mind – identified and attacked a market gap so crassly obvious that one remains to this day wholly bemused as to why no one had spotted it before. His staff – his company – were drunk at the time with the exhilaration of victory, of proving their point.

John Sainsbury, the founder, is said to have had the courage of a lion, matched with a vision of the future for his family business so simple, so clear, so focused, so direct, that nothing and no one could or wanted to stand in his way. He was an elemental force. It was his vision, and his dream. He thought of nothing else. Hilariously really, 'Keep the stores well lit' were reputed to be his last, whispered words to his family on his deathbed. The story is so good that I really hope it is not apocryphal.

Many others have succeeded in delivering an exquisitely focused creative vision. It is happening today, for example, with that fine inventor and entrepreneur James Dyson, whose staff would die for him despite the ferociously demanding, exalted work ethic and insistence on quality that he imposes on them. Imposes? Not really. Dyson is one of a breed whom anyone would follow, blindly almost, given his messianic reach for excellence. Reaching for excellence is a compelling quality of leadership.

Perhaps I have a vested interest in this to get off my chest. At eighteen, I was sick for love of James's older sister, Shanie (seventeen, and to this day every time I see a press photograph of James, so physically like her, I have a jolt in my heart). Maybe she will read this. I gave her a record of Charles Trenet singing 'La Mer'. The sheet music, too. I laid my hand on her shoulder as she played it at her mother's piano. All to no avail. She married an Irish peer, and produced a brood of what appears to be several dozen children.

Dyson, like many of his fellow entrepreneurs (including me), has had his trips to the financial canvas in his time. Quite a few in fact, as many of his early initiatives failed to find their market and his funding collapsed. It is those trips to the financial canvas that provide a point of common identification among entrepreneurs and, unlike in other parts of the community, a consequent lack of censure on those who, however momentarily, fall. As has been said, the entrepreneur's way to look at failure is this: it is the occasional price of success. Or, alternatively, it is the precursor to it. Either way, fail, shake yourself down and get back to business.

One extreme and famous example of a near wipe-out prior to brilliant success would be that of the Barclay brothers, now Sir David and Sir Frederick, who in the mid-seventies defaulted on a debt of £9.5 million to the Crown Agents, and almost lost everything. They survived, barely, and what happened thereafter is an extraordinary tale. An equally extraordinary story lies around Michael Spencer, the all-conquering City entrepreneur, who today runs the world's biggest inter-dealer broking firm, Icap. Spencer's career calamities in his early years, before he broke through, are mind-boggling. He was fired at least twice before he was thirty. On one occasion, with his family's money, he shorted in a major way on gold, and watched, aghast, when almost the next day the Soviet Union invaded Afghanistan and the price of gold rose from $200 to $800 an ounce. Spencer is an adventurer on a quite exhilarating and brilliant scale, like a swashbuckling nineteenth-century merchant prince. Reputedly charming and disarming one moment, awesomely hostile and difficult the next, his personal fortune now approaches £400 million, and he is the richest self-made man in the City. He will end up, I predict, like Andrew Carnegie before him, giving every brass farthing of it away to charity. He is exactly of that stamp.

There is a feature of those entrepreneurs who have stumbled, yet emerged victorious, that I find very attractive:

their notable aversity, in their development years, to spending money on the trappings of luxury that surround conventional corporate life. Trappings waste money, and entrepreneurs are not interested either in wasting money or in trappings as a barometer of success (see comments about Terry Green on page 124). How could they be? The dream has not yet succeeded. For many of his early, dangerous years, Richard Branson ran his office from his home. But my favourite example is Harry Stratford, these days one of Britain's most successful entrepreneurs. Stratford has the headquarters of ProStrakan, the Scottish pharmaceuticals company, his latest venture, in a Portakabin. Earlier he was the co-founder of Shire Pharmaceuticals, the £3 billion FTSE 100 pharmaceuticals company. There is not one jot of flash about him.

We will talk about funding, and the vicissitudes and trials of using the venture capital houses (and then, unless one is careful, promptly being manipulated by them) later on in the book – but suffice to say now that James Dyson is a very strong personification of tenacity, courage and focus, all wrapped up with a healthy contempt for the orthodox, particularly the orthodox financial establishment. He does things his way, and he does them alone. He is not always the easiest of men perhaps, but he is most certainly a winner – and by that I am not referring to his now colossal fortune, which may or may not mean much to him, but to his wholly indestructible spirit.

'Success is ninety per cent failure' he has said. 'You galvanize and keep yourself going, as a full optimist. But it is not just perseverance that counts. It is hope. Hope is the most important element in success. You have to bounce back. Bounce back when everyone else would say OK, I have had enough, and stay on the canvas.'

There is hope, then. Add to hope three other inherent characteristics of every great entrepreneur who ever lived. As Jeremy Bullmore has put it, reacting in *Management Today* to a reader's quest for advice as to whether to stay within a conventional corporate career or to branch out on his own: 'The very fact that you are torn in two leads me to suspect that you are not one of nature's entrepreneurs. Are you possessed of an unlimited self-confidence, a ruthless streak, and an almost manic ability to shrug off a whole series of apparently terminal setbacks?' To that last point I would add: do you have a stamina in you that defies normal limits? Do you have that ability to come back and back, always, whatever happens, sticking to the task and staying in play? It is just that – the resilience every time, all the time, in fair weather and foul, to stick it out and stay in play – that brings life's wins. 'Eighty per cent of success is showing up,' as Woody Allen put it.

We could be a little more prosaic and MBA about it all, perhaps, and recite another business-school mantra, such as the one that the three keys to the building of a successful new entrepreneurial organization are: having a market focus, having tight financial foresight (i.e. cash-flow budgeting and planning for capital needs) and possessing the ability to assemble a top management team. But Bullmore is right.

Those qualities he lists are not necessarily nice, but they are what we have got. The true entrepreneur – the real article – will show that 'manic' ability to defy many setbacks, all at the same time, which in other eyes would appear terminal. They will be ruthless in the attainment of their aims. They will possess a form of self-reliance and confidence that can be beyond the rational.

As we see with the Barclay brothers. And they, incidentally, are a very good illustration not only of the Bullmore 'list', but also of the way all entrepreneurs, once well known, move in and out of favour. The truth is that there is not very much the Barclay brothers can do about that, and the same applies to all of us. The trick is not to worry about it. Ignore it both ways. (Remember Kipling . . .) Jeff Bezos, CEO of Amazon, was *Time*'s Man of the Year – absolutely top of the heap. He then became subject to stories about insider selling. On top of that the Amazon share price nosedived. His braying laugh, once thought endearing, was now described as annoying. Give it time, of course, and the whole business will swing full circle, and that Bezos laugh will be considered to be a thing of schoolboy charm once more. (Writing about Jeff Bezos reminds me that at the time of the millennium *The Times* ran a feature titled 'Yesterday's Men and Tomorrow's Men', and wanted to include in it a picture of me as 'Yesterday' and Bezos as 'Tomorrow'. I managed to stop them. Yesterday's man indeed . . .)

I said just now that entrepreneurs possess a form of self-reliance and confidence that can be beyond the rational.

Optimism – perhaps the coarsened version of James Dyson's 'hope' – is an absolute prerequisite. A true entrepreneur can only see eventual victory. I have that mindset myself, but optimist as I may be, I realize that if you are a rounded enough person you know that life is not only about victory. You may think only about victory, but life is also, inevitably, about defeat (albeit temporary, you hope). So life is also about the dignity and grace you manage to show in the acceptance of that.

'Optimism tends to succeed, but does this refute the majestic truths of pessimism?' John Updike has asked. I like this question because it brings me up short and reminds me that pessimists can be nearer the real, quintessential truths of life than us instinctive, unstoppable optimists. But all of us are as we are. And – well, if you are of the same mindset as me – be grateful that you can sleep at night knowing that however dire the situation you will beat it. That does not necessarily indicate that you are of sound judgement, and it most definitely does not indicate wise maturity. Nor depth. Level-headedness – absolutely not. But it does mean that you have been given the very best chance of eventual victory as an entrepreneur.

And actually for any of us – business people, artists, administrators, politicians, whatever we are – if we are to be content we have to believe that we are capable of significant achievements. And the fact that those achievements, for most of us, really have to be reached out for, makes them all the more valuable and satisfying. People of extreme ability may occasionally, with very little effort, stumble upon an action or an initiative that grants them lasting fame, but the truth is that they often achieve less in their lives than the rest of us. We people of comparatively lesser ability measure precisely the ability we have, and use it to the very last of our being.

And we welcome opposition. It is a hostile world, and few will give you favours, except in their own interests and to their own agenda. We know that. The opposition is there to beat you to the ground, and will try to do so the moment they realize that you are a threat to them. That is neither how it should be nor how it should not be, merely how it is. One day you may perhaps find yourself trying to do the same to an upstart aiming at you. You may, however, feel it encumbent on you to draw up a little short of Ghenghis Khan, who, when his generals said to him that the greatest thrill in life was falconry, is said to have replied: 'You are mistaken. Man's greatest good fortune is to chase and defeat his enemy, seize his total possessions, leave his married women weeping and wailing, ride his gelding, and use the bodies of his women as a nightshirt and support.'

A recent DNA study across Asia shows just how great Ghengis Khan's good fortune was. It is estimated he has about sixteen million descendants.

There is always opposition, and there are always a dozen reasons why your business dream will not work. Perhaps it is the economy. Perhaps it is the sector. Perhaps it is the scorn of the first few 'experts' to whom you have shown your plan. Perhaps it is other people's futurology as to where the industry might be going. Perhaps it is the 'advice' of yet another arrogant, obtuse banker. Listen to too much of this, and it can eat into your soul. So do not listen to it. Expose yourself to it – you must certainly do that – but do not believe it. You have your dream, you are transfixed by its brilliance and its certainty, you know the market, you know the freshness of your vision, you know and understand your numbers, and you know it will work. So – do it.

I used to serve as a non-executive director on a certain board. This company's chief executive was intelligent, technically proficient and persuasive, but – in my eyes – sorely hesitant and indecisive. He once announced to us at a meeting, proudly looking around the table and sure of his applause, that he was 'risk-averse'. Most of the other board members nodded wisely and glanced approvingly at each other. 'Risk-averse' – very sound, that chap. Gravitas. I put my head in my hands. Petulant of me, perhaps, but it had followed several meetings where he had made similar remarks, and this in a company that in my eyes had grown rich, fat and complacent, and the aggregate of it all had begun to irritate me.

What went through my mind at that moment was this: there was not a single great business in the world – not one – that had not been built from the foundation stone of the bravery of its founder. His or her bravery not to be averse to risk, but to embrace it. To look risk in the eye, measure it, but then put it to one side, move on and make the dream work, however long it might take.

All of which, incidentally, is rather what I feel about the collapse of the dotcom bubble. Yes, the bubble burst, but does that really carry the significance popularly ascribed to it? Guru Tom Peters would say that what we actually saw there was intense expansion followed by intense contraction, but the game survives and the best people will stick with it, take the risks, hold their nerve, and in time they will make it work in ways that none of us can currently foretell. One thing that you can be absolutely sure about is that the Internet will surely evolve but never go away. Our moment now is an extraordinary time of uncertainty and redefinition within the technology world, but from this eventually there will be as many huge winners as there are currently huge losers. Those potential huge winners are going to have to show a good deal of stamina, courage and ruthless self-confidence, but eventually they will make it. I hardly have to point out that some have already done so on a spectacular scale.

But let's return to that risk-averse chief executive of ours. What I should have told him was that he would never have been in the overpaid job he occupied had the original founder of that business not taken quite overwhelming risks in his time to get that fine and important company on the road. But move on the decades and what happens? Risk-taking, adventure, intuition, creativity and vision have become to that company's directors terms of corporate irresponsibility.

Mothercare was rather like that. Under several subsequent ownerships the creative vision that the founder Selim Zilka had executed so exuberantly was badly coarsened and dumbed down. The magic was lost, self-doubt was every-where, and the company nearly failed. And family companies, once the founder dies, so often have a similar tale to tell, if few perhaps on the scale of Sainsbury's. In future generations the vision is diluted and corrupted and the passion of the founder becomes transmuted into aggression, which is by no means the same thing as passion.

The second John Sainsbury ruled not through personal magnetism and vision, as his father did, but by rage and by bullying, or so his contemporaries are prone to say. Under his rule the first seeds of Sainsbury's decline were sown. Colin Southgate, recently executive chairman of EMI, could be said to have been of similar style. But bullying achieves nothing, except for a toxic mix of resentment, repression and syco-phancy in your staff. The legacy the bully leaves behind him in his company is the destruction, perhaps for a generation or more, of corporate creativity and momentum.

Bullying is a corrosive force. And hasn't it shown? From overwhelming market dominance Sainsbury's now have been walked over, at least for the moment, by the brilliant, brutal drive of Tesco. And EMI, from being 'a national jewel' in Colin Southgate's words, have declined to the point that they seem to do little else these days but issue profit warnings, nurse their collapsed share price, pay each other quite dis-gracefully large bonuses, and cast around for someone from overseas to tuck them away in a merger and put them out of their collective, passive misery.

Thorn EMI they were, before the apparently boring old

Thorn was spun off and away by Southgate, to leave the hidden jewel of EMI in unsullied, sparkling isolation. But as it turned out there *was* no hidden jewel. The market – chumps, the lot of them – had bought the story that the music business, all on its own, would be a diamond, and the share price was ramped up wildly in the run-up to the demerger. When the split from Thorn was finally accomplished, however, shareholders discovered the Southgate EMI jewel was paste. If that.

Bullying is a corrosive force, but that aside, it is corporatism at its worst that is too often the successor in the generations following the founder's single, focused vision. Confused objectives appear, and with them a further negative: the tendency, or, more pointedly, the compulsion to over-manage. Over-management: the corporate style whereby initiative, creative responsibility and proaction is jealously, tightly guarded within the club of executives at the top of the tree, who then project out a myriad of pluralistic management initiatives to make them feel in control. Over-management can be the death knell of everything.

For me, Greg Dyke encapsulated precisely this when, having been at the helm of the BBC for a matter of only a few weeks, he was quoted as saying that he had never been in a corporation anywhere in his life which was 'so over-managed, and so under-led'. It is a nice distinction: 'over-managing and under-leading'. Leadership is not so much about managing staff as about raw commitment to the articulation of the vision. People follow that. Over-management kills the focus.

For example, dwell on Anita Roddick for a moment, at her peak with Body Shop one of the most brilliantly successful woman entrepreneurs Britain has ever produced. The idea behind Body Shop was so good, so simple, and yet the concept alone – on such a small scale so easily copied (she would say counterfeited) by others – would have been nothing had it not been for her fathomless self-confidence and chutzpah.

In a way Roddick fooled us all with Body Shop, and its peppermint foot rubs and seaweed shampoos and the like. But we all got caught up in the boundless enthusiasm and fun of it. And Roddick really was, and is, a stunningly compulsive motivator, aided by a flair for personal publicity that almost self-parodies.

In Body Shop's prime she carried the self-confidence of the company on her shoulders and thrived on it. The staff, devoted to her, had believed that whatever Anita's dream might be, it always came to pass. They had total faith in her judgement and her decisiveness. She made life absolutely simple, and absolutely clear. But, with the share price slipping, she was told that the company must grow up and away from her, and that she needed to introduce a team of more conventional business executives to move it forward. So the team of conventional business executives arrived, and with them the full regalia of attitudinal researchers, market segmentalists – the lot. And the moral of the story is this: suddenly – for the first time – there was corporate self-questioning. And with the self-questioning came the self-doubt. And with the self-doubt came a sudden rush of fear and a sense of vulnerability. And with that sense of vulnerability came a raft of problems, not least from a guerrilla group of troublemaking franchisees from Europe.

Little vulnerability in James Dyson, of course – to me, incidentally, one of the breed of 'auteur' entrepreneurs, someone whose entire oeuvre, from wheelbarrows to carpet cleaners, is somehow of a piece. And there are many others: David and Luisa Scacchetti of Mamas and Papas, Christian Rucker of The White Company, Linda Bennett of LK Bennett, James Heneage of Ottakar's booksellers, Vijay and Bhikpu Patel of Waymade Healthcare – all entrepreneurs who had and have a vision, believed in it without one quiver of self-doubt, and drove it through.

'Whenever a friend succeeds, a little something in me dies,' said Gore Vidal, and typing in James Heneage's name above made me think of that . . . He had a go at Waterstone's and in many ways succeeded, to the extent that he has now lost his company to HMV, these days Waterstone's parent, who found it wise to take Ottakar's out. But (says he through gritted teeth) I hold my hand out to him as one of the sort who carry their companies on their backs by the sheer momentum of their self-belief, uncluttered, coarsened or diffused by a cordon of 'professional' managers around them.

Laura Ashley too; less the entrepreneur, perhaps, but a brilliantly creative voice. It was her death that did it. No one's fault, but, when she died, suddenly her company's self-confidence, and with it the ability to change and adapt to a radically altering market place, fell apart. It has never recovered, and probably never will.

A company's sense of self-confidence is a mysterious and fragile thing. Great entrepreneurs and their businesses carry self-confidence that is inviolate, whatever disasters may strike (remember James Dyson's vicissitudes in his earlier years, from which he emerged blissfully unfazed). That self-confidence imbues the lives and morale of everyone working with them. Take it away – take the entrepreneur away – and everything crumbles and dies. Difficulties, problems and dangers arise that had never surfaced before. Entrepreneurs have tunnel vision. They have their vision, and they are going to win with it.

The issue of the brilliantly creative voice brings me back to Greg Dyke. John Birt's aspiration for the BBC to be 'the best-managed organization in the public sector' was trashed by Dyke – 'that wouldn't get me out of bed in the mornings' he chortles – and few now would blame him for it. (To be fair, though, Birt does still have his defenders, especially, I have found, in the Civil Service, who feel that Dyke never tried to understand the particular responsibility of a public sector broadcaster of the BBC's unique status. And it must be said that the BBC was indeed abysmally managed in the conventional sense over the period immediately before Birt's arrival.)

Dyke's goal, in pointed contrast to Birt's, was to make the BBC 'the most creative organization in the world'. Though not necessarily himself a particularly creative man, he recognized – vitally for those who worked with and for him at the

BBC – the absolute imperative of freeing and empowering the creative capacity in an organization where the quality and brilliance of the product – the broadcasting – is actually the only thing that matters. To achieve his objective he set eight new demands of the BBC staff (Dyke's Rules, if you like, though they were not known as such):

Inspire creativity everywhere

Connect with all audiences

Value people

We are the BBC

Just do it

Lead more

Manage less

Make great spaces

An entrepreneur's checklist, if ever there was one. I like it very much indeed. If not a great personal vision of creativity, it has the real strength of putting right at the top of the list the need to relish and empower creativity in others, and then be led by it. Everybody has to deliver, embrace the culture, take part. Right down to the cleaners, I am sure Dyke would claim. Birt's management layers slashed, the dreaded 'internal markets' ditched, and everyone empowered to show what they can do, make mistakes and grow. It must have been heady stuff in a depressingly dispirited corporation probably more vital to the cultural and educational good health of

Britain than any other organization. Show what you can do. You are capable of anything. Reach out. Grow.

I think of the early Waterstone's as I write of Dyke in this way, and embrace him for it. My style, absolutely. One of Dyke's biggest targets was the 'them' culture. He had noticed that whenever anything went wrong at the BBC people blamed 'them'. There is no 'them', he says. The BBC is 'us'. There is nobody out there stopping staff doing things; there is only the people who work here. 'Cut the crap,' his yellow cards said. 'Make it happen.'

Greg Dyke, at least from his public persona, certainly had unlimited self-confidence and the ruthless streak. He is a leader. His was a good analysis of the BBC. We will see now whether he has the entrepreneur's ability to shrug off a setback. And remember that the true entrepreneur – the genuine article – will bounce back from a whole series of setbacks, which in other people's eyes might appear terminal.

There is a Jewish joke I have always liked. Moishe, a tailor with a nagging wife and daughters to marry off, is on his knees complaining to God of his poverty and the way it is always other people whom God allows to solve their problems by getting rich and winning the lottery. Always others. Why not him?

'Give me a break, Moishe!' God says. 'Buy a ticket!'

Two

TRUST IN YOUR VISION

Where there's no vision, the people perish.

Proverbs 29:18

Many of the great global corporations of our time should have that verse from Proverbs as their motto – and should be living to achieve it. It is so difficult for the big corporates though, and so easy for the entrepreneurs. Big corporates do not really do vision. The entrepreneur does little else. It is the vision that brings the win.

To have the opportunity to make a real personal mark in the world is the greatest of privileges, and, through vision, that honour is within the entrepreneur's grasp. But remember that even the most successful of players is going to be remembered in the end for just a little cluster of wins. When you have a win in your sights therefore, be absolutely certain that you do not waste it. This will be one prospective win among the very few that your life will offer.

There has to be absolute clarity of vision. Simplicity of vision, too. And that simplicity and clarity can only arise when the founding entrepreneur has a real personal grasp of the industry he is entering. It is no good having a dream of opening a new and wonderfully original chain of restaurants if you have never been in the restaurant business and have no experience of what works in that industry and what does not.

A cobbler sticks to his last – the entrepreneur must stick to his core competency. If it is restaurants you know – then create your dream within the restaurant world. If it is book-shops – start your bookshops. If it is magazines – stick to the magazines.

Simplicity of vision is everything. That is helped by an avoidance of pretentious management speak. One example: you do not find the great entrepreneurs agonizing over the writing of mission statements. Those great entrepreneurs of ours would take the view that if it was not absolutely crystal clear to everyone – staff, customers, suppliers, bankers – what they were about and what they were aiming at, they had failed, and dismally so. Can you imagine Philip Green spending time chairing a committee to write a mission statement for Arcadia?

Kate Swann, newly arrived as WHSmith's CEO, removed their old mission statement from their website. It was, as you can imagine, state-of-the-art blather about WHSmith's role in the community. She replaced it with a nice crisp objective on the lines of becoming an ever-improving bookseller, stationer and newsagent. Easier said than done, but the intention was right, and well done her. My favourite mission statement ever, was written by John Cassell – founder in the nineteenth century of the publishers Cassell's – a chain-smoking Non-conformist from Manchester, whose mission it was to save the working classes from liquor by giving them books, magazines and bibles. Cassell's mission statement was: 'Satan trembles as he sees / Bibles selling cheap as these.' To the point – no?

It is a private game of mine to go into big companies' portentous and grand websites, and read their mission statements. The more devoid the big corporate may be of commercial and entrepreneurial drive, the more splendiferous and grandiloquent – and pretentious – the mission statement. You can only imagine the hours teams of well-meaning people have spent in committee rooms writing the wretched things. They are probably still there, mulling over the next draft.

Take BT's website. It contains vast amounts of information, but so little that is truly of use. For example, an important statistic for someone who is seeking to indicate that BT's share price is undervalued is the number (prodigious, I believe) of mobile phone customers they have worldwide. But search the website, and it is not there. What is there is a mission statement, which wheezes:

> BT's strategy is to build long-term partnerships with our customers. With their support we aim to maximize the potential of our traditional business – through a combination of enhanced quality of service, creative marketing, innovative pricing and cost efficiency – while pursuing profitable growth by migrating our customers to new-wave products and services such as ICT (Information and Communications Technology), broadband, mobility and managed services . . .

And, believe it or not, they are only just warming up. They go on. And on. It is worthy, it is true, but it is all too much.

And it is too little focused. The BT website and the mission statement are of a piece: the picture they give is of a company obsessed with its public service past ('the first coin operated phone box was installed in London in 1906') and very confused about its commercial future. This may well be an accurate reflection of BT's actual culture, but that culture is not right, and it is surely not an image that BT should publicly present. They make fools of themselves in doing so. Clarity of intent for the future is everything. Simplicity of thought for the future is everything. Lack of pretension and obfuscation is everything. Take Vodafone:

> We are enriching the lives of our customers, helping individuals, businesses and communities be more connected in the mobile world.

That is it. Period.

And remember the history of it all. In 1983 Vodafone and BT (Cellnet) were the two bidders who were awarded the original mobile licences. Vodafone was really no more than a thinly capitalized start-up, while BT was one of the biggest, most powerful companies in the world, with vast assets and a virtual monopoly on the UK telecoms market. Look now, twenty-three years on, and Vodafone has whipped Cellnet's butt out of existence. Forget Cellnet. Vodafone's market value is now over £100 billion, no less than five times as much as the whole of BT in aggregate.

It really is an astonishing fall from grace. BT should have led the world. It had looked for a time as if it would do so.

Its early rivals in the rest of Europe cowered at the prospect that the lean, mean London-based innovator would be unleashed in their markets. But far from leading the world, BT became in time a laughing stock, overtaken not just by its counterparts in France and Germany in terms of market value, but even by the Spanish. BT became a byword for managerial incompetence, spending more time worrying about their position in the community, and to whom they should extend their sponsorship largesse, than in selling telephones.

'There is no such thing as society,' Margaret Thatcher famously pronounced. There *is* such a thing as society, actually. Society exists, and it is what binds us together, and government and civil and cultural leaders are there to protect and nurture it. But BT's society – any business's society – is only a contained world marked by parameters. It adds up to just this: its society is its product, its reason for existence, its customers, and its staff. Add, further down the list, its shareholders and its suppliers, and that is it. Vodafone knew that, and BT did not.

Vodafone has been a stunning story of raw entrepreneurial drive. The fast, nimble, driven and committed David, set up in competition against a ponderous corporate Goliath.

Today is a particularly opportune moment for fast and nimble newcomers. The incipient failure of merger mania gigantism leaves the market wide open for the fleet of foot. A feature of the *real* new economy is its inherent fragmentation. Giant corporations are not very good at inherent fragmentation.

In the Western world, disposable income is growing inexorably larger – and moving upmarket. As it moves up-market it seeks ever more personalized service: customized, organic, genuine, handmade, anything but the mass-produced or computerized. Personalized, customized, handmade – these are fertile areas of operation for the start-up entrepreneur. And the real new-economy businesses tend to be labour intensive. The work is flexible and often local. Catering now outperforms the entire manufacturing sector. Add leisure, entertainment and tourism and you have Britain's biggest employer by far.

As Simon Jenkins of *The Times* has written, unlike manufacturing – inherently if not inevitably the territory reserved for the corporate giants – the real new economy enjoys status among young people. A cult economic thesis has long held that the future will only require 'knowledge workers', an elite of cyber-surfers and financial wizards, leaving behind an unemployable, rebellious rump of computer illiterates. Like Jenkins, I believe nothing will prove further from the case. The outlook for the new economy – the entrepreneurs' economy – is measureless. Personal services call on human skills, and the satisfaction of working for oneself or in small groups. Success can be most simply measured – even to the level of counting the day's takings. And unlike most of the e-economy, these businesses have an excellent shot at making money.

*

I think there is no doubt that the death of conventional capitalism is in the air. The classic capitalist economy is one in which the factors of production – land, labour, capital – are combined in the pursuit of producing goods and services to be sold to consumers. In their time the providers of capital, banks and the banking system were the cornerstone of everything. But now what we are seeing is the onset of something different: a consumer-driven society.

Land? Labour? We had 'Fordism', a management approach typical of capitalism in the early- to mid-twentieth century – uniform products for consumers who did not complain at lack of diversity – permitting an overwhelming management focus on maximizing resource utilization. Double Diamond – Ind Coope's truly awful production-driven fizzy brew of the 1960s or so (now, mercifully, expired) – was a good example of that. The brand was marketed with colossal marketing and advertising support, with the objective of squeezing out and destroying the consumer's natural propensity to search out for the idiosyncratic real ales, which was where the genuine consumer market lay. No one knows this better than me. To my embarrassment I have to confess that I was a junior marketing man in the company at the time. Very junior. It was not my fault. I still pretend to myself that I put up a paper wondering if we were doing the right thing.

Capitalism raised people's living standards, and fuelled the consumer-driven society that followed. The relationship between capital and enterprise has fundamentally shifted in favour of the latter. The new depositories of the Western world's economies' most important resources have become individuals, and collections of individuals. Sources of capital have become two a penny. People are precious.

So, individualism and authenticity are all, and what could be more fertile ground for the entrepreneur than that? Big corporate brands are suspect. The biggest of all – Levi's, Kellogg's, even Coca-Cola, certainly McDonald's – are drifting out of favour. 'The flat wilderness of standardization', as Chesterton called it, is anathema. People now search for organic vegetables with the soil still on them. Bespoke olive oil from some obscure little Tuscan village. Dressing down in khaki is 'authentic'. Mountain bikes are 'authentic'. The Lush stores, with the great cakes of hand-hewn soaps sitting there on counters of Provençal-style butchers' blocks, are 'authentic'. And sometimes the 'authentic' is all the more attractive if it is a little bit vulnerable, a little bit flawed.

Perfection can be a turn-off. Do you remember Freud and his 'narcissism of small differences'? The key for the entrepreneur today is to invent something 'real', and lift from it the essence of its desirability. Lose the negatives, but sometimes keep a little hint – a charming little hint – of the unstable, the amateurish and the vulnerable.

And when you have deduced by intuition the essence of the product's desirability to the public, do not second-guess it. You have pressed a button. You have got a winner. Play that essence of desirability back to them. Spin the hell out of it (which we certainly did in the early days of Waterstone's). It will be a product that people never knew they wanted until they saw it. When they do, they will flock to it. Mobile telephones were the perfect example of that. Remember and draw a lesson from the barmy market research that wholly misidentified their potential.

Fear your competitor – or your apparent competitor – not at all. Have in mind that a lot of the time we all tend to regard our competitors as being the key players in our own precise trading sector. Fearing those people may actually be quite irrelevant. We cannot really know who our competitors are. Waterstone's, for example, is probably competing for each pound the consumer spends not so much with other bookshops as with alternative ways of spending intelligent, culturally aware money on an urban, wet Sunday afternoon – a movie perhaps, a gallery, a concert. There is really not much Waterstone's can do about that, except try to be a very, very good bookseller. Similarly, the Blackberry may compete more with newspapers and magazines for the bored business traveller's time than with other brands of handheld devices. Now, goodness knows if that particular example is true or not. In some instances and with some people it will be, but in many others it will not. Life does not break down in such a simple form, for Blackberry or anyone else. Life, and people's actions, are all too prolix. That is the point – they are too prolix to research meaningfully, and to do anything worthwhile off that. Do not worry too much over something that you can have little insight into or control over. Just do what you do. Your only defence is to do it absolutely the best you can. And the only way you can do that is to have an instinctive, wholly reliable eye for what, in your consumers' eyes, actually rings the bell. Once again, intuition is the one and only way through. And intuition is what entrepreneurs do.

It is a good time for entrepreneurs, and while we have mostly been looking at the most famous and flamboyant, the real heroes may not be famous at all, but any man or woman who starts a serious business, takes the early, potentially devastating personal risks, and wins, builds the business up and sticks with it for life. When all those years later retirement finally has to come there is a turnover of – what? Fifty million pounds? Hard earned profits of – what? Five million pounds? And over the years hundreds, perhaps thousands of staff have had happy, honourable, fulfilled working lives, pensioned into their retirements, supporting perhaps four times their number within their families.

To extend that point, I feel that all entrepreneurs, of whatever personal style, have one characteristic in addition to those one might expect to find (huge self-confidence, ruthlessness, an ability to ignore setbacks): a profound, perhaps paternalistic, perhaps sentimental attachment to the people who have got behind their leadership and given them their working lives. It is a great driving force. As we will discuss later, the sheer accumulation of money is not in any way the be all and end all of the battle, whatever might be popularly supposed. Winning is what it is about. Just winning. Risking it all, and losing, never complaining, and starting again. Proving the dream. Winning for the whole team.

People who understand the risk, measure what they are

doing, and then do it: these are true heroes. Salute them. People who have made their dream survive and built decent, solid businesses are heroes who have fed more into the community and provided more good things for more people than any government initiative could possibly hope to do.

Well – you too are going to do it. You are going to join them. You are going to take the plunge. You are setting off on another stage of your life's journey. For, as an entrepreneur, you really do have to think of your life as being a journey: always in progress, always teaching you as it goes. Failure in one thing and adversity within another are all grist to the mill, the counterbalances, no more than that, to the moments of sudden success and happy, perhaps surprised, good fortune. There is luck in it all, but the luck does seem to even itself out over the course of the journey. And a certain humility – not meekness, and absolutely not a lack of self-confidence, but humility, a willingness to learn, a lack of arrogance goes a long way.

This is a big moment in your life. Maybe you have been shuffled out of a corporate establishment to which you have given your best for years. Maybe that has happened, though, because you are not really a corporate animal at all and, however hard you have worked, that has showed. It has showed perhaps in your body language in what you perceive to be tedious, rambling meetings, or perhaps in the short fuse of your e-mails to the corporate bureaucracy, the people who seem to be there only to encumber your life with needless, fussy communications. A short attention span when you think your time is being wasted is typical of entrepreneurs. Bill Gates dropped out of Harvard University. Why? For no other reason than because he was bored, and impatient to get on with what he thought of as being real life. Michael Dell was a dropout from the University of Texas in Austin for exactly the same reason.

It is going to be nerve-racking financially, but you have persuaded yourself that you are ready for that. The counter to the financial stress is that you are going to be *free*. The economy at that moment may not be perfect, and interest rates high, so the timing is not ideal, but that is what you have got. And at least your new company is going to be operating within an industry you know a great deal about, which is exactly how it should be. Best of all, most exciting of all – it is this that keeps you awake at night in blissful anticipation – your idea is one that taps dead on to what you know intuitively to be an unmet demand within that market.

It is high time you did it. You have consoled your nervous wife or husband with the thought that a cyclically depressed economy can be the perfect time to test one's entrepreneurial mettle. You have nearly persuaded yourself of the same point. And at least there is one thing: at the very worst, the experience of having to pitch your business plan will deepen your network, and teach you lessons that will hold you in excellent stead when you go back to the job search. Actually you have no intention of going back to the job search, ever, but that sounded very responsible and mature when you said it to your partner. And it succeeded in reassuring and rather impressing him or her, at least for the present.

But you are reading this book, and in your darkest moments you still question yourself. It is good that you do, for if the entrepreneurial life is not for you, you really must not touch it, or there will be calamity. Ask yourself those questions that you really do have to answer: how strong and 'different' is your vision? How good are you at motivating and leading others? Do you really have enough experience within the market you are entering? How brave and resilient will you be when things go wrong? Can you deal with extreme, relentless financial stress? Is there a streak of ruthlessness within you? Are you prepared, and brave and self-confident enough, to use that? From whatever personality source, do you truly carry an intense desire for personal achievement?

Do not fool yourself about one single aspect of this. Without any doubt you will have to put up a personal guarantee against every penny of your new company's debt, so your house, which will have been mortgaged up to the very hilt to enable you to invest in the business, will be the first thing on the line if the company wobbles. Realize that the banks will not hesitate for one second to call you on that, and at the first hint of trouble. They will call the loan in, and give you very little time indeed to honour it. There are children in that house of yours, I expect, and a spouse. What about them if the axe falls? Would your marriage or relationship survive that? Could you cope with the damage you are inflicting on your children's security?

If the financial risk of it all obsesses you – and why shouldn't it? – absolutely do not do it. Please – do not do it. Settle back down into corporate life and stay there for the rest of your days. Enjoy whatever friendships and camaraderie you can find in that, and – why not? – milk the personal benefits, not least the comfort and protection of a good service contract and a decent pension. There is nothing wrong with those things. They are good. So, quite without hesitation, let that be your life. Please, do not try to be what you are not.

But let us say you pass test number one (if 'pass' is the right way of putting it, which it is not . . .). You have thought it through all over again, and you are absolutely certain that what obsesses you now is the opportunity. We will say that again. It is the *opportunity* that obsesses you, not the *risk*. You recognize that obsession with the opportunity is a fundamental of the entrepreneurial mindset.

That is all in order, then: the opportunity you have unearthed quite obsesses you; you have calculated the amount of money you are going to have to raise to get the business off the ground; you cannot wait to get started. You are ready to go.

That is excellent. But stop there for a moment. The first thing you should do now is take your plan to five or six people in the industry whose opinion you feel it might be good to hear. Do not fool yourself – each and every one of these people will tell you not to do it, and explain why. But while ignoring their advice (and you will do that) it is a good idea to listen hard to what they are saying. You are going to swim against the stream, because that is what you believe in, and that is your mindset. Swimming against the stream is the thrust of what your business plan articulates, so it is going to be very useful indeed for you to hear the opposition out. Let them spell out for you where and why their cynicism is focused. That may annoy you, but it is also going to help you. Think of it this way: these gurus, in their negativity, may actually serve to lead you, by accident, to an area you may have missed, where you can achieve even more than you had thought. They will be delivering received wisdom to you. Maybe there is an area of the received wisdom that is even more flawed than you had initially identified. And if the gurus' perception is that the whole industry you are intending to enter is terminally, hopelessly, in a state of doubt and muddle, then particularly prick up your ears. Markets in terminal states of doubt and muddle are where the newcomer often thrives best; the entrepreneurial genius lies in spotting opportunities that others cannot see. (Steve Jobs created the personal computer when virtually everyone around him doubted it would work, and told him so. Kodak rejected their employee Chester Carlsson's vision around photocopier technology; Carlsson left them, and founded Xerox.) Remember too that the huge leaps in life often stem from the most simple actions. Entrepreneurial triumphs are actually not all whizz-bang moments of startling creative epiphany. For example, it has been argued that it was not the discoveries of penicillin or insulin that made the great advances in health care; the real advance lay in something much simpler: the clean-up of the water supply. The magic lies simply in spotting – by intuition – the real need. Visionary grandiloquence has nothing to do with it.

I personally went through the guru-subjection process when I was planning Waterstone's in 1982. There were good precedents in the book world. One story is always told by George Weidenfeld with great relish. Before starting up their company, which became one of the great publishing houses of the world, George and Nigel Nicolson asked the legendary Jonathan Cape for advice. He suggested that they met over lunch. They found him extremely disagreeable, even before he advised them, sternly, that a publisher's profits could come from only one source: strict economies. They must never, ever forget that. He then proceeded to order for himself the most expensive fare that Claridge's could supply, and left the young partners to foot the bill.

Well, I took my business plan to my industry 'experts'. We did not meet over lunch. I told them that I was going to build the biggest bookselling group outside the US, and the best anywhere. (Such modesty, with exactly £22,000 available in my drawer for equity, but there we are . . . Of that amount £16,000 was, perforce, borrowed from my then father-in-law under an usurious deal – I was obliged to repay him with £55,000 not so very long after. What a business-man . . .) This industry guru number one – head in those days of perhaps the most famous family bookselling firm in the world – explained to me that it was impossible to recruit good people into bookselling because if they knew anything about books they would only wish to go into publishing. Because of that conversation we promptly hardened our plans to hand complete authority to branches over the range they held. That way our booksellers could immediately demonstrate their personal book expertise both to me and to the public, and take the plaudits for it. Thus – feeling themselves empowered and appreciated – we would keep them.

Industry guru number two – head of a big literary publishing house – explained to me that it was a hopeless time to be thinking of doing what I wanted to do. Booksellers' buying margins were about to be put under a severe squeeze from publishers. The common little men (i.e. the booksellers, as shopkeepers they were artisans of course, while publishers were the gentry) could do nothing but say thank you and accept the crumbs that would be offered, otherwise they would not be allowed any stock to sell at all. The result of that was we adjusted our plan so that it now showed not static but radically accelerating gross margins as we moved forward. We realized that we were going to be the only people opening bookshops rather than closing them down. And we would be opening as many bookshops as we could lay our hands on, and as fast as possible. And publishers would realize that if they wanted to see those stores opened, then in the interests of their authors' books they would have to help us. And realise too that we were not mice, and we would be perfectly ready to say boo, and that if they wanted our shops to be opened then they would have to offer us good margins and decent credit terms. And that is a battle, incidentally, that still rages.

Then on to industry gurus three, four and five. They all were creatures of the message that the book was dead and nobody went into bookshops any more, so – just forget about the whole thing. I had been to my first Booksellers' Association annual conference, and heard exactly this view, hyperbolically delivered. I can hear it now. The opening address of the chairman to the massed audience: 'The English are illiterate, ignorant and crass,' he thundered at us, a furious, plump, flushed, gesticulating figure.

> They cannot read, they will not read, and there is nothing we can do about it. We must face up to it. We – literary folk, publishers, authors, agents, booksellers – are fools. And we are fools living in a fool's paradise. The book is dead. The book is finished. This is an illiterate nation. What we have to do is accept that, come to terms with that, put it behind us, and get on with our lives!

Something like that. Magnificent stuff. The Booksellers' Association delegates loved it. He got a standing ovation.

So you have seen the industry 'experts', you have rewritten the plan in response, often in direct antithesis to their received wisdom, and now you need to raise the money. But pause again. It is not just a question of how well you have articulated your dream. Nor is it only a question of whether you have the messianic courage to take the financial risk. It is going to be a question too of who you are. You have the guts, yes, but ask yourself this question once again: do you have the leadership within you to pull this off? Do you have – there is no better word for it than the overused one – the charisma?

Yes, charisma. The term originated in theology. It referred to a talent given to a person by God as a free gift or favour, which, coming from God, leads others to be attracted to it. More than that, it leads them to follow full-heartedly, even blindly, to obey the leader willingly and affectionately, to feel an emotional involvement in the mission. We have coarsened and secularized the term since then, certainly, as we have applied it to our contemporary political and commercial life, but the essence of it remains. Charisma is about leaders articulating goals and values – preferably, but not necessarily, good goals and values – and those leaders leading followers. Leading them by dint of personality and charm, rather than any form of external power or authority. Heroic feats are attributed to leaders with charisma. The charisma that paints compelling visions of the future, inspires passionate, persuasive belief in the leader's vision, relentlessly promotes the leader's beliefs. The charisma that is the fountainhead of creative ideas, and the inspiration of extraordinary performance in others – partly by giving them confidence in themselves, and partly by giving them faith, and belief, in their leader.

All that is fine, but in the wrong hands charisma can be dangerous – nowhere more so than in politicians, we would all agree, but it has to be said in business leaders too. It is not blind fanaticism in the service of megalomaniacs we are look-ing for. It is not the acquisition of power only for personal gain and exposure. Those things are charisma at its worst. Charisma at its best provides the sort of leadership that coaches, develops and supports the team of followers, shares recognition with them, enlarges them so that they feel independent, confident and personally capable, and gives them the room to take responsibility for their own actions. And, with their leader, establishes a set of internal ethical and moral standards to guide their actions and behaviour.

All of this can be achieved in a hundred different ways and styles. What is certain is that it is not necessarily bombast that is required. Bombast, noise, shouting – these in themselves do not contribute to charisma. Harry Truman, who many would argue was one of the three or four most effective presidents the United States has ever had, might be said by some to have possessed not one ounce of charisma in his being. But that would be charisma used in an unduly narrow sense. What Harry Truman represented, indeed personified, was bland, small-town, conservative America – a Wal-Mart man if ever you saw one. But he was loved and respected and faithfully followed by all who worked for and with him. Why? Because he was an absolutely rock-solid, cast-iron, unpretentious man of trust. Those qualities, properly presented, can be intensely charismatic in the eyes of followers.

Truman was much in the mould of a personal hero of mine, Britain's first post-war prime minister, Clement Attlee (Truman's contemporary in power of course, and maybe, in a world that was at that moment exhausted by war, there is a kind of logical symmetry in that). When Attlee said yes, when Truman said yes, yes was what it was. When they said no, it was no. And the important thing was that they never gave conflicting messages on any issue to different interest groups. The style was dead straight, take-it-or-leave-it honesty, demonstrated, in both men's lives, by a most affecting and genuine modesty. (I am particularly attached to the story of Attlee, just a few days in power, wandering out of Downing Street into Whitehall one pleasant evening to catch a bus home to his wife in North London, pursued, too late, by sprinting security officers.)

I believe that the two men's trustworthiness, allied to their affecting modesty, added up to a most powerful charisma to which others associated themselves most readily. There was a hint of something similar in Ronald Reagan, whose charisma was based on relaxed, folksy charm certainly, but this matched up with a most focused personal recognition of what he was intellectually capable of, and what he was not. This kept him, and America, out of a lot of trouble. And in business leaders, perhaps most particularly in entrepreneurs, such reliable self-awareness is priceless.

Following the Ronald Reagan example, you must never fall into the trap of pretending to have expertise when you do not – that is not at all where charisma lies. Why do that? Hire expertise in those areas, and give the experts room to work and a reason to follow you. Build on your strengths – and know with absolute certainty what those strengths, as much as your weaknesses, are. The one strength that you must have, the sine qua non, is the ability to persuade and to inspire. Exactly as Reagan succeeded in doing, in his folksy way, with America.

It is true of course that persuasion can come in many different forms. But whatever those forms might be, they are greatly aided by a talent for delegation, by allowing people their heads. 'Empowerment' has become a buzzword in contemporary management speak, and because of that it is perhaps now parodying itself, and thus losing its edge. (And, God! how I loathe management-speak. 'Low hanging fruit' is my current *bête noire*. That and 'best-in-class'.) Allowing staff the freedom to use personal space and initiative to make their mistakes on their way to making their triumphs is indeed essential to entrepreneurial success – but they really do need to know what is going on. Here's another of Sam Walton's rules:

> Communicate everything you possibly can to your colleagues. The more they know, the more they will understand. The more they understand, the more they will care. Once they care, there is no stopping them. If you do not trust your associates to know what is going on, they will know that you do not really consider them partners. Information is power, and the gain that you get from empowering your associates more than offsets the risk of informing your competitors.

However, a word of reality around this. The chief strategist of an organization has to be the leader – the chief executive, or the executive chairman, or, if they are true partners together, of truly common mind (and are perceived as that by their staff), then both in tandem. A lot of current business thinking has stressed the notion of empowerment, of pushing down and getting a lot of people involved. That is very important – more than that, it is vital – but empowerment and involvement do not apply to the ultimate act. That ultimate corporate act is one thing: choice. Successful entrepreneurial companies work because they have a very strong leader who is willing to make choices and define the trade-offs. Look around you. Look at the big corporations and you may have to look quite a long way before you find that quality of leadership. Look at the entrepreneurial companies and you will find it all the time. Good leadership provides good strategic direction. The one leads inexorably to the other. Best-selling business visionary Tom Peters is right as well, of course he is; as he never stops saying, it is wonderful people that make wonderful companies, and that is all there is. But those wonderful people are most truly empowered not by 'freedom' in itself, but freedom within the parameters of a company with a strategic vision so clear and articulated that all can understand the joy of working within it.

The leader has to make sure that everyone truly understands the strategy. Ask around, listen, and be absolutely certain that this is so. Strategy used to be thought of as some mystical vision that only the people at the top understood, but that violated the most fundamental purpose of a strategy, which is to inform each of the many thousands of things that get done in an organization every day, and to make sure that those things are all aligned in the same basic direction. If people in the organization do not understand how a company is supposed to be different, how it creates value compared to its rivals, then how can they possibly make all of the myriad choices they have to make? Every salesman has to know the strategy – otherwise, he will not know who to call on. Every engineer has to understand it, or he or she will not know what to build.

Harvard's Michael Porter, currently probably the world's most esteemed business school professor, says that the best CEOs he knows are teachers, and strategy is at the core of what they teach. They may not call it strategy as they teach it, but teach it they do. They go out to employees, suppliers, customers, and by their actions and their body language say, 'This is what we stand for. It is a very simple thing. It is a very different thing. This is what it is.' They repeat it endlessly, teach it endlessly, to the point that everyone understands it.

In great entrepreneurial companies, Porter says that the strategy becomes the cause. It does so because it is about being different. If you have a really great strategy, people are fired up. They will come to believe that you and they are not just another bookshop/toyshop/airline. What we want to bring you, Mr Customer, Mrs Member of the Public, is something new. And it is ours. We are bringing something of our own. We are bringing something different, and worthwhile, and it has got our stamp on it, and we believe in it with all our hearts, and it will add good things to the lives of all who deal with us.

But it is not always a perfect world like this, of course. Sometimes the freshness runs out of the most charismatic businesses, and everything starts to feel blocked and stagnant, needing a good flush through. I'll tell you what has worked for me in the past when this sort of situation seems to have settled in: as the cliché goes – regard it as an opportunity, not a threat. Sit down with the team for exactly one day – a long day with a minimal lunch break but concluding with an extremely good dinner in an excellent brasserie (a cheerful, humming brasserie so that there is a minimum amount of oppressive formality, and a maximum effort at fun, laughter and the feeling of victory and problems faced up to, analysed and resolved). Run the day yourself – 'facilitate' it yourself (more truly dreadful contemporary management-speak). It will be all day, so the challenge is to keep the energy and concentration levels, including your own, very high indeed – and, vitally, to ensure that every individual contributes fully. Use a small, cramped room for maximum interfacing. Run the day like this: give yourselves just one hour to break the company's activities down to its constituent parts (maximum of nine or ten of these: 'our customers', 'our product', 'our reputation', 'our staff', etc.). Then take say three hours (up until lunch, and no one eats until this part of it is done) to analyse those constituent parts down to individual sub-issues that need formally addressing. After lunch, allocate chiefs who will be personally responsible to you for each constituent part, and agree together how each of the sub-issues are to be addressed (this will take three or four hours of solid debate). Set a date to meet for the reporting-back process, not more and probably not less than one month on. Then – that is it – set off for the brasserie. And when you have that meeting four weeks on, make sure that you emerge with an absolutely clear, simple strategy on each issue. Again – once more off to the brasserie, and make sure that the following day, by the afternoon, everybody has a copy of your summary of what has been agreed (it is vital that you write it yourself, so that you can personally tidy up within the summary anything which the next morning still looks woolly).

This sounds automated and orthodox, but it brings us back to the art of inspiration. Sometimes quoted in this context is the example of the queen bee. Charisma, in whatever form it comes across, inspires the conditions that foster openness and the release of energy in others. The queen bee is not there to make decisions, but what she does do is to emit the chemical substance that holds the whole society together. What leaders do by their charisma is strengthen human bonds by binding everybody together into a society with a single common purpose. Everyone is inspired, and they are trusted (because they are inspired) to perform to the best of their ability.

Every person, at some time, has a desire to be an achiever. For many, this ambition is destroyed. Under a true leader, this latent desire can come back to life. I am not sure I want to push this queen bee analogy in entrepreneurial life much further – Anita Roddick a queen bee? – but let's just say that she (the queen bee – and Anita too now that I come to think about it . . .) does her job so effectively that the worker bees have the elbow room to do theirs. And they, the worker bees, get – must get – the credit for it.

It is interesting to watch a charismatic leader working the room as they move from person to person. Bill Clinton, whom I have physically witnessed at the job, is spellbinding, but I do acknowledge that great political leaders are in a way too easy to use as evidence of this (though I have to say that at the particular occasion I am referring to, at a small reception at the University of Warwick five or six years ago, Clinton was accompanied by Tony Blair, and the difference in style was illuminating: Clinton all pause, calm, slowness, and sudden, delighted laughter, his hand gripped on elbows, and his schoolboy-crooked tie, and to each and everyone his searching, almost loving, eye contact; Blair all pancake make-up, damp forehead, wandering eyes, rictus grin and impatient bustle).

It occurred to me then, watching Clinton, that charisma can work better than anywhere in small groups, and best of all, one to one. The person being talked to, even if it is just for a minute or so, can receive so much attention and care that they feel that to the leader, at that one moment, they are the most important person in the world. As a person. As a human being in their own right. That is charisma. That is leadership.

I am going to tell one story from my own family's history

before we move on – and I will tell it because it illustrates to perfection, to me at least, the true genius of intimate, one-to-one, inspirational charisma. Leadership, if you will, in its purest sense.

One of my eight children is adopted, my much-loved Maya. She came to my family from India, just a very few weeks old, a baby from Mother Teresa's orphanage in Calcutta. Maya learnt from us as early as she could absorb it where she came from, and was of course enormously proud of it, as well she might have been. Nine, ten years old, her bedroom was full of press cuttings and pictures of Mother Teresa. One day we read in the newspapers that Mother was in London for a few days, staying in the convent of her Missionaries of Charity in a remote corner of North Kensington. Maya saw this and wanted to see her, but we imagined it would be impossible, such was Mother Teresa's fame, and her commitments.

We called the convent, however, explained that we had in the family one of Mother's orphanage children, and how much Maya longed to see her. We asked if something, however fleeting, could be arranged. Maya's mother was allowed to take her to the convent straightaway that afternoon, but when they got there they were warned that Mother, deep into her final years by this time, of course, had gone to her room to sleep, and that the nuns wanted to leave her undisturbed until the early evening. They were allowed to wait, and then, eventually, there was the sound of voices and bustle at the top of the staircase, and there was the tiny figure of Mother

Teresa, one of her Sisters whispering something in her ear. Mother turned and came down the staircase with her arms extended, a broad smile across that wrinkled, iconic face. Maya stood and waited for her at the bottom of the stairs, wide-eyed, smiling too. Mother Teresa reached her, and hugged her to her, then, still holding her by the waist, stood a little back and looked deep into her eyes.

'Do you remember Maya, Mother?' one of the Sisters asked. 'Remember Maya?' she replied, incredulously. 'How could I ever forget Maya? She has, she always had, even as a baby, this . . . light of God in her eyes.' Then she held her to her once more, briefly, laid her hand on her head, and was gone.

Mother Teresa was lying through her teeth of course. Babies by the thousands, tens of thousands possibly, had been born at her Calcutta orphanage in the interim. Maya had been there only for a week or two following her birth, and while there she had been temporarily assigned a different name altogether. How could she possibly remember her? But it was a superb act of leadership, of inspirational humanity, of pure genius. It had taken no more than a few seconds of Mother Teresa's time, but the effect she had on my child by what she had done, the gift she had given by that, was priceless. It was a thing of lifetime balm. And it amused me then, as it amuses me now, that even a great saint, for surely Mother Teresa was that, found no difficulty whatsoever in telling a wholesale lie, cheerfully, in the greater good of performing an act of quite wonderful kindness and power.

Well – if you are to be a true leader in your great venture, and truly charismatic, you will need to dwell on these things. You may not be planning to build the biggest company in the universe, but you are planning to build something worthwhile, a business of good values, and are possessed by a strong sense of purpose and mission. You may not be naturally effusive and bombastic, but – and this is often misunderstood – you do not need to be that. Shy men and women, provided that behind that shyness is a combination of real steel and real warmth, can be as charismatic as anyone, and, because it is more subtle and complex, perhaps the more so. People of this sort often train themselves up to be highly successful public speakers, for example, realizing that they will need to do that, given their natural propensity for reticence. Once they have mastered their fears and reached a level of genuine competence, their more discursive, retained style can be very effective indeed. Incidentally, whatever your personality, you should train yourself up to be a highly competent public speaker, as the skill will hold you in very good stead, and the techniques are not difficult to acquire. In public speaking as much as in private conversation, whether you are naturally effusive or a little reserved, the key is to be true to yourself, and to present yourself as you really are. As Noel Coward said, the one thing that your audience has to have is absolute, rock-solid confidence in you the moment you step on the stage – the certainty that you are not going to embarrass them by inadequacy in your performance. You have to learn how to give them that confidence – and it is so much easier to do that if the persona you are presenting to them is the persona that you truly have.

That applies to everything you are going to do, and not just public speaking. You cannot achieve anything unless you are confident in yourself, and sure of your self-esteem. And you cannot be sure of your self-esteem unless you are sincere, articulate, focused and respectful of the people who are following you.

In a recent survey of more than fifteen hundred managers (the UK Department of Trade & Industry report of December 2004), people were asked what they would most like to see in their leaders. The most popular answer, given by 55 per cent of people, was 'inspiration'. When asked if they would describe their current leader as inspiring, only 11 per cent said yes. The two attributes that people actually mentioned most often when describing their leaders were 'knowledgeable' and 'ambitious'.

That survey makes my point exactly. 'Knowledgeable', 'ambitious': it is not these attributes that followers yearn for in their leaders. It is charisma. It is inspiration. That is what you are going to set beside your courage, your ability to live with risk and stress, and your desire to put all that into this great new dream that you are going to turn into reality, for yourself and your team. The team will reach out to you, if you can provide that inspiration. Maybe we have not drifted so far from the original theological definition of charisma after all.

Three

TRUST IN YOUR LEADERSHIP

Ever tried. Ever failed. No matter. Try again.
Fail again. Fail better.

Samuel Beckett

Can inspirational and charismatic behaviour be learned, or is it only an instinctive gift? I think it is possible to learn these qualities, but only if the desire to is really there, and if the learning of it does not take forever. But, as we have said, it is a journey. A journey, and not a destination. Passion is indeed everything – you really do have to believe in what you do – and passion is a continuing journey too. You can believe in bad things, of course, but it is my view – not perhaps the popular one – that most effective entrepreneurial leaders do in fact combine passion with moral awareness.

Putting the question of moral awareness aside for one moment, acquiring and demonstrating the skills of charismatic leadership are actually often a matter of being in exactly the right place – for you – at exactly the right time – for you. Put in charge of a mechanical engineering business, and you might well be hopeless. Put in charge of a music publisher – your passion in life – with the resources to let that passion thrive, and you might well be outstanding. Your passion, if you give it full rein, will enable you to be as tough, and as relentlessly single minded (to the level of ruthlessness), as you will need in order to be a true leader. You need to be ruthless, we have established that. Passion will generate that in you. Passion is what progresses life, and it is what will attract wonderful staff, rescuing themselves from their embedded dissatisfaction arising from their big corporate careers.

No one wants to be part of a corporate team they do not themselves believe in, and why should one be in it for all, when the 'all' is not in it for them? The importance of an organization's purpose, and connecting employees with that purpose, is not rocket science. In entrepreneurial companies that connection is easy. Maybe the corporates spend too much time talking about strategy, when strategy does not really matter beside the need for every member of the team to be infused with a sense of common purpose. Professor Sumantra Ghoshal has argued on these lines in the *Harvard Business Review*. He said that in companies founded and led by entrepreneurs the articulation of a sense of common purpose is second nature. But what is second nature to the big corporates is to have their central focus in organization. As the entrepreneur's company emerges into maturity, the perfect match – so hard to achieve – was the two second natures grafted together.

We can put that another way. Let us agree that entrepreneurs are, as a breed, right-brainers (creative and intuitive). However, perhaps they do best when they have somewhere on their team a reasonably powerful but by no means dominant element of left-brainers (analytical and logical). These attributes are neither correct nor wrong – but it is the right-brainers who make the world zing. It is the left-brainers who are supposed to save a catastrophe or two en route to that.

Corporations are entirely left-brainers, sometimes to the point of excess. Take the Royal Bank of Scotland. It's in their tradition, and I am not berating them for that, but they have these days so left-brained their lives that, present them with a major corporate project (and their rule is to pace big corporate initiatives and projects so that a team cannot start on a new one until another one has finished – can you believe it?) and you are in for some heavy programming. I think we can take it that there have been some management consultants in that office . . . The theory is that they will time their corporate projects in such a way that they are scheduled to come to resolution after a multiple of thirty, sixty or ninety days. Like the conductor of the symphony orchestra, their aim is to anticipate the ending at the beginning, and modulate their performance within that framework. This surely derives from Stephen Covey's *Seven Habits of Highly Effective Persons* (six million copies sold, and counting, so who am I to carp if Covey's 'principles' read to me sometimes like an odd mix of the banal and the crassly commonsensical?).

There is a remarkable degree of discipline within the RBS, and a phrasing and a pacing, and all these things matter. I just wonder, however, whether in their hands it is too much, too rational, too cold. Surely more than a minor element of right-brain zest and pragmatism needs to infiltrate the process at some point. Where that is going to come from is another story, but come it must. That is the endemic problem that every large corporation must try to address. The virtuous circle closes at the magical point where left-brain rationalist influence on right-brain creative brilliance means that the left-brainers enable the corporation to make serious money from the right-brainers' intuitive flair. I say that rather piously. It is orthodox business-school-speak. Privately I am wholly on the right-brainers' team. Can I whisper it? Left-brainers – who needs them?

You will find right-brainer, inspirational, charismatic leaders in all walks of life. You will find them in both the private and public sectors. You will find them in charities and schools. You will find them in big businesses and small, early stage ones. These stars of the entrepreneurial world can come in all shapes and sizes – perhaps as reserved Truman clones, perhaps as colourful, noisy backslappers – and all over the spectrum in terms of their strengths, weaknesses, cultural values. The palette is so wide, and so full of variance. Wherever you find them, however, their characteristics will resemble each other in many ways. They have a vocation. They have followers. They inspire people. They achieve through others, and they achieve for others.

We have discussed the mindset requirements already, of course. The need for a certain ruthlessness in the discharge of a very clearly articulated and inspirational vision. An almost insane ability to absorb stress. An instinct for containment within areas where the founding entrepreneur has a high level of personal competence and experience. A desire by him or her to accept personal responsibility for all major strategic decisions and the communication of them. A focusing of everyone's minds, not on difficulties, but on the central opportunity at which the team is aimed – and not just an opportunity in cold, commercial terms, but a vision; a great aspiration. We might add one more characteristic – a short attention span! I have never met an entrepreneur with anything else. That is both a good and a bad characteristic. It does at least enable the entrepreneur to cover a tremendous range of work over the course of a day.

The big corporates can develop at least some of these mindsets – at least, sort of develop them – if they are properly led. I like what I read about John Cleghorn, CEO of another great bank, the Royal Bank of Canada. His style of leadership is unusual for someone in his position in that type of institution. He is very involved in the operational details and standards of the bank. He has been known to call from the airport to report that an automatic teller machine is not working. He sold the corporate jet his predecessor had acquired – he said he just was not comfortable with it – as well as the chauffeured limousines, and he has introduced a very structured yet imaginative regime. All senior executives, including Cleghorn himself, are expected to spend 25 per cent of their time with customers and frontline employees, and they formally and personally measure that week by week. The bank's stock ownership plan has helped almost 90 per cent of employees to become shareholders. And, what is unusually interesting, senior executives must as part of their employment contracts personally buy – not merely have an option –

out of their own resources one to two times their basic salary in stock, with Cleghorn himself obliged to buy and hold at least three times his salary. Not one hint here of the soft world of stock options – these people have to pay for their shares upfront, and hold them. The amounts at personal risk are not inconsequential.

This is good leadership, and rooted in a very practical and direct way. I admire it. But the right-brainer in me, in counterbalance, always wants to consider team leadership in a more romantic way. I like the concept sometimes expressed that leadership, in whatever walk of life one finds it, has many different facets. It can be deeply practical, as with John Cleghorn. It can be a softer thing, reaching followers mostly on an emotional level. At my most extreme, I would say that real leadership is not really about feelings or emotions at all; it is about the spirit. Look at others and you can glimpse yourself, for we are all of one family. When you reach the autumn of your days, as I have now (very early autumn, of course . . .) that becomes so clear, it really does. Why are these truths obscured from one in youth?

We are all of us members of one family. Leaders have that gift of identifying and reaching out to the vision of greatness they see in others. It is good to believe it is there, somewhere in us all, maybe not to Hollywood scale, perhaps under a narrow focus, but there nevertheless. Greatness. As John Buchan said: 'The task of leadership is not to put greatness into people but to elicit it, for the greatness is there already.'

Thus the great dream moves forward, and the team is

built. And thus the team remains on course, with full optimism. Actually, to make the point a second time, something better, less coarse, than optimism. As James Dyson said: hope.

And the team is what it is – a team – and the entrepreneur not only takes care to say 'we' rather than 'I' when there are good things to announce, but also means it. This point is so relevant and so important. Of course it is the founding entrepreneur, the dreamer of the whole edifice, who privately tends to think (if careful not to say publicly) 'I' – after all it is he or she who took and is probably still taking the burden of immense personal financial risk in getting the business off the ground. It is vital, however, that the word disappears entirely from the screen when it comes to describing the positives. It is most important never to lose hold of this discipline. Every success, every good initiative, every win must be 'we'. Every failure, every piece of bad news must be 'I'. Once again: wins are 'we'; failures are 'I'. Stick to that rule as you build your business. It works – but only if you mean it. Make yourself mean it. Be proud of your team. Hire the best people you can, and be proud of them. Shield them from criticism. Protect them from failure. Hand the laurels of success straight to them. Accept for yourself the guilt for failure.

This links in with the issue of the founding entrepreneur taking responsibility for decisions, and particularly decisions about hiring staff. I personally feel very strongly indeed that you should make it an absolute rule to embrace that responsibility. Do it yourself. It is not the HR people who should be hiring, it should be you. (HR – 'Human Resources' – is to me such an offensive term – management-speak at its worst. Though 'Human Capital' is I think even worse.)

As you do your recruiting, remember that the only management model that will ever succeed for you is one that is based on people's freedom, and respect for their need for gratification through work. You really do have to carry an absolute belief that people *need* work. They need it for their sense of self-respect, and sense of honour. You must feel that it is a privilege that you can provide that for them. And you must despise the negative put-down that people are lazy, and that the whole lot of them – particularly the blue-collar people – want to come into work as late as possible and leave as early as possible and make more money than they deserve. In a happy company that is never, never true. What you must believe, and as an entrepreneur I am sure you do believe, is the reverse of that: if you allow people respect, freedom and self-propulsion, they will thrive. By freedom, though, I do not mean anarchy. Freedom to customize their jobs a little, and express themselves in their own way. Freedom to have a view and talk about it. Freedom from the boarding school mentality of silly rules around silly shibboleths. Anarchy is something quite different. Anarchy is indiscipline and a dishonest lack of open-handedness. Freedom makes people happy. Anarchy makes them totally miserable. Never confuse the two.

Samuel Smiles – author of the Victorian mega-bestseller *Self-Help* – compiled hundreds of mini-biographies to make a single point: true success and happiness can be achieved only through hard work, perseverance and self-restraint. Noel Coward's aphorism 'work's more fun than fun' (I have always liked that very much) is in the same vein. Smiles is right. There are no quick fixes. There are no cheap and easy routes through. Smiles's aim is to show that many of those people whose lives seem so effortlessly successful in fact owe their success to years of hard work. Hard work plus an enlightened sensibility and a meditative temperament. A realization that all of one's life is connected, and of a piece. Smiles recounts the tale of how Sir Isaac Newton, when asked by what means he had worked out his extraordinary discoveries, replied, 'By always thinking unto them.' And Sir Joshua Reynolds, when asked how long it took him to paint a certain picture, said, 'All my life.'

These days Smiles, if he is heard of at all, is dismissed as the arch priest of a selfish, competitive individualism. That is not fair. He denounced the worship of power, the goal of wealth for its own sake, and conspicuous, soulless consumption. For him the real aim of life was to develop character – but character for a purpose. For Smiles, the only true tests of character were the degree to which we commit ourselves to life and the manner in which we conduct ourselves towards others. How can one disagree? Is there a better test?

People of real status yearn for the dignity and sense of honour that hard work brings. They are attracted to life within entrepreneurial companies because of the emphasis placed within those companies on personal commitment, and the expectation of empowerment.

Human Resources departments tend to take a backstage role in most entrepreneur-driven companies. And for a good reason, in my view. People decisions are much better taken by those who are closest to the people, and who thus both really care about, and have a vested interest in, the result. Recruitment in particular should be done only by those who personally care about what happens – which means, as I have emphasized, the entrepreneur himself or herself, perhaps most usefully in the company of the person to whom the recruit will report.

Over the years I have hired hundreds and hundreds of people myself, and I think the mystique of trained professional skill around the process of recruitment is much exaggerated. One has to accept – and rejoice in the fact – that it is a very flawed, imperfect business, and one much more dependent on intuition than science. (There we go – intuition again . . .) On the one hand, the company lies about what a wonderful place it is; on the other, the candidate omits important information about his or her faults. How it will all work out is very hard indeed to predict, but the chances of success are enormously improved if there is a proper cultural fit between the two parties. That – a good cultural fit – is one of the factors that interviewers should be looking for above everything else.

For that reason as much as any, I personally find it unforgivable if the responsibility for recruitment is sloughed off, particularly in the early years of an organization's life. You, the founding entrepreneur, above all others, will have a feel for what a proper cultural fit actually means, and this matters so much. So, I repeat: hire your people yourself, and as far down the organization as you can reach in practical terms. Because you have personally hired your people, you will feel a real sense of responsibility to them, and for their happiness and fulfilment in working with (not for) you as part of your team. If someone fails (and many will) take the view that it is your failure as much as theirs; you had read their ability and skills wrongly, and should not have exposed them beyond or outside their weight. That is the ultimate unkindness actually, let alone inefficiency: asking anyone to operate beyond their range. (A public example of this is the unfortunate British politician, Estelle Morris. Personally so praiseworthy and idealistic, she, perhaps uniquely, resigned from her Cabinet ministerial post because she realized, in time, that she was not up to it, and that the department – education – was too important to trifle with. Her resignation was a most honourable act, but it has now finished her as a politician.)

Never be too busy to spend time and energy, as your business builds, in getting the right people into the right jobs. Set the example yourself: delegate freely and confidently to others work they can and will do better than you. Tell all your people to do the same, but by delegating they have to understand that they are *not* absolving themselves from personal responsibility. Emphasize that to them, and tell them also that all the management must follow the company's golden rule, as you are determined to do yourself: it is worth saying it again – if and when in the future there is good news, then the joy around that is 'we', and if and when there is bad news, the blame and the responsibility is 'I'.

The best entrepreneurial companies do two things simultaneously: they treat everyone in the company quite excellently, but they are totally tough and uncompromising in what they want from them. The company is tough, but at the same time the company is kind. Inspiring, visionary leadership flows from the painting of a dream. It is the dream that moves people to follow you, you respect them for that and treat them well because of it. It is the dream that inspires, never the numbers. Not money. Think twice before even mentioning the numbers. Stick with the dream. The dream is where the charisma lies. Numbers have another context and purpose altogether, and not much of it elates. The old Hollywood joke: 'You just *have* to see new movie X. Why? They brought it in on budget.'

If you are going to do the hiring, you are going to have to do the firing. That is good. They are mirror images of the same responsibility, and of the same privilege. The classic advice over firing cannot be bettered, and one should never deviate from it: when you are obliged to send people on their way, give them total respect; give them courtesy; give them time; give them fairness; and give them total, unambiguous clarity. I say this because what seems to me to be a new and by no means desirable trend is the way in which some highly publicized staff lay-offs are being carried out now in the biggest corporations. A lot of top managers seem to enjoy the cruelty, and the macho male aggression of it. The public bragging around staff dismissals is wholly despicable. An example would be the comments of the chairman and chief executive of the largest trade publishing house in the world, Random House's Peter Olson, in a scathing July 2003 profile in *The New York Times Magazine*. In the preparation of the profile he was followed around the BookExpoAmerica convention in Los Angeles by NYT reporter Lynn Hirschberg. '[Olson] kept pointing out former colleagues and chortling "I fired him" and "I fired him". Many of the "hundreds of people" he recognized at BEA "I fired personally", Olson added happily. "There are so many people here that I've fired that we could have a reunion."'

I felt ill when I read that stuff. If we are in an era in which you are a hero in a big corporate if you take pride in cruelty to your staff's sensibilities, then that is an abomination.

As you recruit, build the team and settle the company down for the big adventure, one thing that is very important is that you should think through your salary structures most carefully. It sounds too obvious a point, but if these are initially inaccurately and carelessly set, salary planning and implementation can cause a ton of trouble down the line. J. P. Morgan, who certainly cannot be accused of disliking money in his day, gave an order to his investment people never to put money in a company in which the chief executive earned greater than 30 per cent more than the next layer of management. That chief executive, he said, cannot build a team and the company will be inevitably mismanaged. He also dictated that the proper ratio for salaries between the top people and the rank and file should be twenty-fold, post tax. That should be the highest differential. Beyond that you create social tension.

That is quite a radical view, and given that Morgan personally paid himself notoriously well, it should perhaps be put a little in context. But, as in all benchmarking, these differential margins do provide food for thought. The detail and scale may be wrong, but the underlying point has much merit.

In the context of staff remuneration you will also be considering whether to allocate equity or equity options to your staff, and how far down the tree these should stretch. My advice – I have personal scar tissue here – is just pause on this one before you act too hastily. Ask yourself the question and think about it: do your staff really need stock options at all? Do they really need equity? Sometimes it is said that if there are still cars in the staff car park at six-fifteen at night, then that is because they have their go-go options; stand at five o'clock in the evening at the exit gates of the company next door, where no one has access to equity, and you will be trampled to death. But . . . I am not sure. Take the young technology companies, for example, presently beleaguered or not. The truth is I think that the excitement around working in tech is generated not so much by stock options as by the chance of working on something that is cool. There is little bureaucracy. There is little emphasis on administration, or, in young people's eyes, paper pushing, and that is a big plus for them. The tech people are at the cutting edge of new frontiers, inventing a new world and new products to fit it. They are creating the future. Yes, the staff would like equity options if they are offered them, but is there more risk than upside to the company in doing that? What happens when the strike price of the options remain under the water, as it very probably will in today's stock markets? Doesn't this actually illustrate and enumerate 'failure' when in fact everyone has done a good job? What people want, this line of argument suggests, is excitement, fun, bustle and cama-raderie. And bonuses – frequent and really generous bonuses – for specific, individually recognized achievement. Wealth, eventually, as a means to freedom. But options? I am not sure. In a very settled environment, as in John Cleghorn's Royal Bank of Canada, yes. In young entrepreneur-founded com-panies I repeat – I am not sure. Exit-market value coming in under initial expectations, perhaps severely so, can serve to disappoint and disillusion. This downside – a most painful one – must be taken into account. So, as I say, a most gener-ous bonus system, geared as close as possible to the individual contribution of each manager, can be much simpler and much more effective in terms of motivation. Through bonus sys-tems, the pitfalls of disappointing people because of low stock valuation at realization – usually through absolutely no fault of the individual – can be avoided.

Morale is everything, and morale largely springs from inherent attitude. Hire for attitude, train for skill, says the old saw, and it is true. I had an experience at London Heathrow recently with two British Airways employees, one at the ticket desk and the other a steward. The ticket clerk was distant, detached and ignored my smile when I stepped up for my turn. I asked a question, she answered, but in doing so turned away from me and pulled something from a drawer behind her. Now – I am deaf, and if someone turns away from me I sometimes find it difficult to pick out a single word. As she turned back to face me, I apologized, explained that I was deaf and asked her to repeat what she had said. She did so, loudly and pedantically slowly. And, to close, CAN (pause) YOU (pause) HEAR (pause) THAT (pause) NOW?

It was rudeness beyond rudeness, and, shaken by it, frightened almost, I moved away from her to another clerk who had just become free. An hour later I was on the plane, and had the counter experience. I asked a question, some simple question, of a steward, who answered me with such unsycophantic charm and patience and pleasant good humour that at once all was well. I felt completely restored.

The first employee was doing more harm to British Airways by her conduct at that desk than a million pounds of advertising could assuage. The second, by her smiling good heart, was delivering the million pounds of advertising single-handed. When she spoke to me she looked me fully in the eye and for the few moments of our contact, I mattered to her. Believe me, because of my earlier experience, she mattered to me too.

All of us building businesses can learn from that, and stories like it. When it comes to people who will be dealing with the public – maybe every employee – hire, always, for attitude. Attitude – enthusiasm, laughing good humour, bustle, desire to take responsibility – is a jewel without price. Of course you need the skills – I am not suggesting that you employ people without absolutely top-grade relevant experience when you are recruiting for specific roles which require that professional experience and skill level. But always, even then, watch for the attitude first. High skill running with poor attitude will ruin you. One other thing: like singers, actors have a given range. Training can expand it, but not much. The same applies to all people in all situations. People either have the basic ability to do the job, or they do not. Training, in itself, will never be enough. Excellent attitude is in itself, by itself, priceless.

There is one area of specific professional skill that you simply have to be brutally honest about. Everywhere, but perhaps particularly here, you have to fire as decisively as you hire if the incumbent is not up to the task. As probably all of us who have built start-up businesses through their early years will confirm, the most difficult appointment to recruit to a good enough standard is the finance director. Broadly, finance directors are like professional footballers. They will go wherever the money is best, and where the win is most certain. Start-up and early-stage companies cannot afford to pay high remuneration, except in the most unusual circumstances, and any stock options you put on offer will look too uncertain a win in a company so unformed to a finance person's contemptuous eye.

Almost inevitably, therefore, the founding entrepreneur will perforce have to accept in the company's early years a second-rater in the finance function. Motivate them the best one may, lead them the best one may, and they will remain second-rate. And finance is too important a specific, technical function to have in the hands of a person one cannot absolutely trust to be reliable. One black hole appearing without prior warning in the young company's cash-flows, and all may well be lost. Cash-flow black holes are killers in young companies if one has not had the time to prepare remedial action against them. If all is indeed lost, that is a tragedy when your company was born into such a glow of optimism and hope and excitement.

In hiring your finance chief my strong advice – from bitter personal familiarity with the subject – is to err on the side of experience. The occasional battle scar is wholly desirable in your recruit. You can do with an irresponsible young Turk in this role like you need a hole in the head. Find someone who may not be a world-beater – actually they will not be a world-beater as he or she would not otherwise be available to you – but who has been there before, knows the traps, appears to like you and what you are aspiring to, and will not willingly let you down.

That is the best you can do, bar one more thing: make sure you yourself are as savvy as you can be about the company's financial affairs. Most of all, the cash. Have as clear an insight as possible as to how the cash moves through the company and how the cash-flows can be influenced and diverted, for good or for harm. It used to be said that any start-up that promises to have profits in less than five years is a phony, but any start-up that does not have positive cash-flow in eighteen months is also a phony. That is probably too orthodox today – though orthodoxy is no fool, of course. At the most ludicrous moments in the days of the dotcom bubble, very few of the internet start-ups could ever have had a positive cash-flow. They were not businesses. But your new company is something real. Cherish it and protect it. You can do that by never running away from looking at the realities of your present and prospective cash position. Realize that cash-flow is everything, and be proactive master of its planning and application yourself.

So, do be careful in recruiting your finance people. Finance people with a good line of talk and a confident air about them can get almost anything they want, it often seems. Watch them like a hawk. Psychologists have done work around this area. They tell us that a man who is confident beyond his merits is much more likely to be hired than one who has the self-knowledge to align his modesty with his ability. The modest man is, of course, the better choice, and the best and most experienced interviewers will plump for him, for his modesty is usually based on a reasonably accurate view of his skills and the challenges he faces. The immodest bluffer, on the other hand, is a fool and a menace. And a total disaster if in charge of your company's finance. He will misjudge the situation in front of him and imagine himself the master of it. It is you who will pay the bill for that – and it may finish you.

One more point about hiring, and I appreciate that it is a somewhat quirky one. I have a most profound personal belief that women are the superior sex. I love women, I marry them, I find it a privilege to have friendship with them, and to acquire insight into their minds and souls. Pound for pound, I believe they are better than men – equally intelligent but more probing, more rounded, more structured, more hard working, more loyal. I am assuming in this that you are a man – well, hire women into your wonderful new business. Listen to them. Empower and inspire them. They are the people who in effect control the purchase and service decisions of all Western societies. If you reach their imaginations and minds they will provide you with a most superior level of loyalty. Mix the sexes, but use women wherever you are able. The decisions will be better, the productivity higher, the company a happier, more focused, more balanced place.

I am a great believer in the wisdom of Charles Handy. He was extremely kind and complimentary about me personally in not just one but two of his books, so he must be a good man. I am dragging the metaphor here just a little out of the context in which he himself tends to apply it, but – we are back in the queen bee territory – he has a strong vision of 'villages' of people working together in harmony, in common trust, for a common purpose, under a common vision. It is not the cult of corporate efficiency he admires, but togetherness, the satisfaction that can be found through working as a team with a vision to aim for. That goes some way to reach towards Freud's benign juxtaposition in his *Civilization and its Discontents*: 'Work and love are the only ways in which human nature can come closest to happiness, or at least avoid misery.' And love carries a much wider context in this than simply the romantic.

Handy rebels against the increasing pervasiveness of the cult of efficiency in business, rather than happiness, togetherness and achievement. His *Age of Unreason* takes its title from George Bernard Shaw's epigram that all progress depends on unreasonable people, for they are the ones who try to change the world, while reasonable people simply adapt to it. This 'unreasonable' nature of the entrepreneurial mindset is one that we can recognize so clearly: those qualities that do not necessarily make entrepreneurs the most comfortable of bedfellows, but can make them powerfully inspirational as they set out to slay dragons and defeat the forces of darkness.

I mention Handy in this context as corporate structures are on the move – and not before time – and much of the reason for this lies in people's desire for fulfilment in their working lives. In this lies such an opportunity for the entrepreneur. The wind is behind us. Big corporations, indifferent employers of shackled employees, can serve, and generally do serve, to deaden the life experience for their staff, leading to a sense of diminished self-worth. These people are having a dumb life in the corporates, and they can have a much happier life with you – so we entrepreneurs should get out there and steal and rescue the best of them.

We should do that, but we must be realistic in this too, and recognize that for many people – to the entrepreneur bafflingly many, perhaps, but there we are – whatever their dissatisfactions in corporate life, it is nonetheless a relief for them to be able to shelter within the hierarchical, paternalistic environment that corporate life can offer. After all, that environment will probably bring with it their pension, and the return home to their families each day at five o'clock. And – who knows? – that generously priced early retirement at fifty-five. There are those people, and we should acknowledge and respect them. But there are the others too, so many of them – people like you and me – who never can be satisfied or fulfilled in the bosom of big corporation life. People of our sort can only find a sense of achievement at the sharp edge of entrepreneurial business building, where passion, commitment and danger lie.

'Big countries are unhappier than small countries; more responsibilities,' John Updike once wrote. For big countries read big corporations. I doubt there is a single really happy big company anywhere. Let's face it, big corporations can be, on the whole, most unpleasant places to spend your working life. We would think that, wouldn't we? But are we wrong? Look for example at the recent toxic management struggles at Morgan Stanley . . . Happy small companies, however, are legion. Small groups of people with a common purpose and identity, working together against common enemies for the common good – all that adds up to happiness.

The operational and recruitment advantages that big companies historically had over their smaller rivals are mostly all gone. Advantage number one was access to transnational or international funding. Now everyone has such access if one is of the mind and the self-confidence to reach for it. Advantage number two was access to information, but thanks to the Internet information is now everywhere. And actually the smaller and medium-size businesses know more of what matters than the bigger ones. The leaders know every customer and every supplier. In the big corporates you get reports. Reports tell you what someone else thinks you want to know. That is not at all the same thing.

There really is a different climate afoot now. Companies have simply got too big. What is happening is that the very best of the young, educated people no longer want to work in the big institutions. Yes, they want to start there – the prestige, big initial remuneration packages, great training programmes – but before long they want to leave. Why? Because they realize that the big companies provide no more career security than the smaller firms – and often decidedly less. The older generation may be clinging on in there in the corporates, but for young recruits, those good old days as their predecessors perceived them – safe, lifetime, generously pensioned careers – are gone. And, as we all recognize, they are gone for ever. So, if personal security for the young recruits in large firms has gone, why work there, feel yourself to be constricted, and be the object of incessant and malign political plotting? In that medium-size entrepreneurial company, when there is a contract to fix in Hong Kong it is the young recruit that goes to fix it, because it is his or her responsibility, and he or she is empowered to do it, obliged to do it, and he or she likes that, and while they are there in Hong Kong they will have a ball. That degree of empowerment and individual responsibility would typically not be there for young recruits in the big global corporates.

There was an army recruitment advertisement that ran in Britain a few years ago, challenging young men and women as to whether they really wanted to spend the whole of their energetic young lives as cogs in someone else's machine. Cogs? In some awful machine? Of course not. Well, join the army and see the world. I am not sure that advertisement said what it thought it was saying. I think the real answer to the question the advertisement set is this: it depends on the machine. Some machines – team machines, with people working together to a common purpose – can actually be wonderful places in which to spend your days – yes, as cogs. For most people do not want to be stars. They cannot be stars. If well led, they can truly find the greatness within them, but that greatness will not emerge in the form of star billing. They know that. It does not matter. What matters to them is that they want to think, they want to *know* that their work, their contribution matters to the team.

It is very fashionable to talk about teamwork nowadays of course, and it looks so easy: much use of first names, empowerment cells, away days, tree hugging, open plan offices and everyone eating in the same canteen – why, the biggest corporations can be just like a small one! Just guys together! Just one happy family! There is the probably apocryphal story of the factory in northern Japan, where each morning the directors and the staff stand intermingled, side by side, fists raised, to chant 'We must work harder! We must do our best in all things!' Now there's democratic teamwork for you. But in truth habits die hard. Corporations are just too big for that sort of intimacy to work properly. They can try, as Archie Norman did at Asda with his 'Ask Archie' buttons and cheeky, reversed baseball cap. But it is the numbers – the scale of it, the sheer size of the work force – that defeats them. Big corporations simply employ too many people for intimacy to have any texture to it. Texture or reality. There was the famous Percy Barnevik, the messianic leader a decade or so ago of the engineering colossus ABB. He announced that he would set out to meet and greet individually at least five thousand of his employees each year. Rather like the Wal-Mart leaders to this day, he was on the road all week, and in head office only on Saturdays and Sundays. The company and its leader exhausted themselves. Would ABB break first or would Percy Barnevik? He did. After a couple of years of this he stepped down.

As we have said, the sheer size of the big corporates is what causes so much of the problem. Small units simply perform with more focus and more drive, because there is an intimacy between the leader and the followers. It is, for example, interesting now, with the wisdom of hindsight, to look back two decades and more at the 1982 Justice Department ruling that dropped its antitrust case against IBM, but enforced a total break-up of AT&T. What happened next? IBM, too large, too monopolistic in culture, slowly proceeded to lose dominance in every sector they had once controlled – and I mean controlled. They have suffered a quarter of a century of degeneration, both economically and culturally. AT&T, however, pushed into its break-up kicking and screaming as they may have been, experienced a new dawn. Forced into smaller and smaller business units, individual indolence turned into individual passion and commitment. Those units became agile, swift and single-minded. They had purpose.

Corporates are structured around layers of management – multi-layers to which management have for generations devoted their lives in the attempt to ascend the ladder. But what is happening is that the requirement for multi-layers of management collapses under the huge wins we are experiencing now in information technology. Most of those layers of management are information relays, and like any relays they are very poor. Each time the message is passed down and transferred it is coarsened and corrupted. Every transfer of information cuts the message in half. Bit by bit those management layers will drop away, as information and instruction is delivered online. As the famous Professor Peter Drucker, Clarke Professor of Social Sciences at Claremont Graduate University, teaches so emphatically, the new information technology has now practically eliminated the physical costs of communications. This has meant that the most productive and most profitable way to organize is in a sense to anti-organize; in Drucker's phrase, to dis-integrate.

In the future there will need to be only very few layers of management, and those who do relay information have got to be very smart indeed. In corporates the management layers linger, because that is the way it has always been. In entrepreneur-driven companies those layers are evaporating as fast as one looks at them. Faster. And the energy that is released by that is extraordinary.

'We succeed in life only as we identify in life, as in war, or in anything else, a single overriding objective, and make all other considerations bend to that objective,' said President Eisenhower. Eisenhower certainly had his faults, but I like the simple focus and unpretentious clarity this quote encapsulates. Sound strategy starts with having the right goal, and the right goal, the prime goal, should be a cultural aspiration – what Charles Handy would call 'soul' which your company will truly live. Having said that, of course, that articulated cultural aspiration should be backed by something wholly quantifiable in financial terms. That can only really be one thing: superior profitability. If you do not embrace the goal of eventual superior profitability from the start, and seek it pretty directly, you will quickly be led to actions that will undermine strategy.

However, let me qualify that statement. There is a certain crudeness in the assumption that the be-all and end-all of commercial life is to maximize profits, and I am by no means suggesting that this is the case. That is one of the problems with the private equity industry, where actually that tenet *is* the case. All the venture capital people are looking for is the biggest exit valuation they can get on their investment in the shortest possible time – and the crudeness of that wipes out any reference towards the 'soul' of the business they are investing in. Real people – real entrepreneurs – have a dream, and the interesting thing is that the dream is so often positioned at the culturally most satisfying, aspirational end of the market they are entering. Yet the quest for superior profitability has to be made. So, we must seek a balance between defined cultural aspiration and healthy profitability. If your goal embraces quantifiable aspirations other than profitability – to be big, let us say, or to grow fast, or to become a technology leader – you will hit problems unless you are very careful in what you are doing, and in what you are saying to others. Now, the fast building of market share is a wonderful way of getting a large payout on a trade sale to a big corporate rival. That is why WHSmith had to pay through the nose to get access into Waterstone's. It happens all the time. That is demonstrably the case, and it may well be right for you to go for that – but if you do so, know what you are doing. A drive for market share may lead to quite a severe short-term lack of profits. That lack of profits will lead to strain with your banks, and the constant need to replenish the company with shareholders' funds. Having to do that is time-consuming, uncertain and risky. Are you sure you are up for it?

One thing we can be sure of. What you are carrying with you is a wonderful mindset asset, common to all true entrepreneurs. You have the instinct to make all business life as unprolix as possible. Concentrate each year on just a very few, absolutely clear management initiatives the context and importance of which all the staff can understand, get behind and support. With an excess of management initiatives everything becomes a muddle. Go for decisive action. Keep decision making crisp. Keep the centre as small as is sensible – too many people will lead to too many competing initiatives and insufficient clarity. Look to build productivity in each and every member of the staff, concentrating particularly at the lower management levels, where, if you really look for it, you may well find jewels. Avoid like a plague the dreary, fearful, bureaucratic torpor that big corporate life can become. Preserve for all time the fun, bustle and drive – and the humanity – of entrepreneurial companies on the make. And I mean on the make. Determined to win.

It is in keeping it unprolix that the smartest companies, big and small, get such leverage. An example of this is that the brightest organizations all over the world are adopting and implementing personalized, one-to-one consumer marketing strategies – as straightforward as they can make them, and as tightly focused. Take Amazon.com. They allow you to store your shipping and order information on its website, so the next time you order a book you can get it with just one click. It is this principle of convenience of repurchase that is beginning, I am sure we would all agree, to separate the good consumer websites from the poor. If repurchase is easy and service top class, customers stay loyal. Amazon's repurchase rate is now claimed to be 64 per cent. A good conventional bookshop would have a repurchase rate of pretty well 100 per cent, but a 64 per cent strike rate over the Internet seems to me to be a commendably high figure. And I have no doubt it is growing, Amazon's brand values being what they are.

Don Peppers, founding partner of Peppers & Rogers Group, perhaps the world's premier customer-centred management consulting firm, is very strong on this area. 'Take Levi Strauss & Co.,' he said in a recent interview:

> Drifting out of fashion they may be, but they are another class act, with a strong flair and tradition for personalized marketing. When they marketed a programme called 'Personal Pair', a line of make-to-order women's jeans available in an astonishing ten thousand different sizes, they said they experienced a 38 per cent repurchase rate, compared to the normal repurchase rate of just 12 per cent. Again, Levi Strauss made it easy, service levels were exemplary, and their customers flooded back for more.

He also talks about the London-based fund management group Mercury Asset Management. '[MAM] have taken mass customization in the print arena to a whole new level.' To serve its customers better, Mercury, owned by the Merrill Lynch Group, recently released its first mass-customized magazine, *The Mercury Investor's Guide*. This biannual magazine mixes common pages with personalized pages in no less than almost eight thousand versions! They really are very smart at it. For instance, they ran an article on the topic of retirement. For older clients, with more substantial assets, the article covered income protection and portfolio diversification. For younger clients the article discussed strategies for retiring early. This highly sophisticated, painstaking marketing works for all who try it – MAM's customized guide apparently attracted almost one and a half times more business in its first three weeks than the previous generic guide did in four.

So, keep it unprolix, focused and as one-to-one as you can get it. Also, amid all the drive and bustle and passion, keep it calm. Tom Peters – the all-action, all-drive, all-revolution guru *sans pareil* – is a spellbinder, of course he is. Action beats the pants off sitting around and thinking about action. It is always better to try a swan dive and deliver a colossal belly flop than to step timidly off the board while holding your nose. The essence of Peters is this: you won't get anywhere without people. (Not strategy – who needs strategy? – people.) The only way to effect true transformation in the work place is to enlist the outliers in your organization to join your cause. Find the weirdos and the freaks, offer support for the projects they are secretly pursuing, then get them to help you with your own revolutionary change ideas. Under-promise; overperform. Is that Tom Peters in a nutshell? Great stuff. You can hear it from him in person in living colour for – what? – fifty thousand dollars an hour? Worth every penny.

But . . . I remember reading his massive bestseller *Thriving on Chaos* when it was first published, in 1987. (This was just five years into Waterstone's life.) Create more chaos in your company! Mr Peters famously tells us. Then more chaos!! – Exclamation marks by the thousand!!! Then do it again!!!! If it ain't broke – then break it!!!!!

Well . . . yes. At that time I was trying to open a major new store in Dublin. After a long run of great successes, which we had somehow assumed would roll seamlessly on into the future for ever, our most recent store, in Scotland – huge, very expensive to fit, staff and stock – was performing a mile under expectation. The economy had suddenly gone absolutely dead, sales everywhere were slack, and our bank was very uneasy. Through overconfidence, we now found ourselves beyond our overdraft limit. I was increasingly concerned that the bank would indeed bounce our payroll, which they were threatening to do. One of our shareholders told me (and the other investors), that they would not support an emergency rights issue to plug the cash gap, so I could forget about that. I had developed a sinus abscess so painful that the only way to cope with it, and work, was to rinse my mouth out every few minutes with tepid water – nothing else would touch it. The Irish unions were encouraging the builders fitting out the new store to demand daily cash sweeteners from us, or walk. Or worse. (And 'worse', in Ireland at that time, meant getting a fire bomb dropped through your skylight, which is what eventually happened.) Our brand new mail order division had clearly failing software, and we were losing track on who had ordered what, and – disastrously – whether or not they had paid us. A famous politician's mistress was suing us for a million pounds because one of our biggest branches had failed to removal from the shelves a book on the politician which defamed her.

Tom Peters – what I needed was *more* chaos? I would *thrive* on that?

I appreciate that what Mr Peters is saying could have theoretical value, perhaps, in big corporations, monoliths that need shaking out of bureaucratic inertia, the British Telecoms of this world, the General Motors. Maybe. There are some interesting ideas in his Liberation Management, of course. If by 'thriving on chaos' he is exaggerating for dramatic effect on our own 'swimming against the stream', then in a way I am with him. With his plea that staff, all competent staff, however junior, should be empowered and listened to, I absolutely agree. But to developing entrepreneurs my personal advice (which I am willing to make available in person at a striking discount on Mr Peters's fee . . .) is less furiously aggressive and apocalyptic. Be subservient to no one and to no received wisdom. Trust your intuition. Think for yourself. Have moral values. Give a crystal-clear sense of direction. Be brave. Lead through inspirational example. Above all, create a business which by virtue of its spirit and originality and sheer quality will survive. Keep in play. Get to the winning post of a secure future. Get there. Finally – make it.

Chaos is the last thing you need when you are building a business. You need a calm mind, a clear vision and highly supportive staff. The staff will be supportive because they want to follow you and they want to follow your dream – because you so clearly believe in it and now they do, too. If there is change afoot, development of the founding idea, then that change should be controlled, disciplined and methodical. Methodical, disciplined – those are not Tom Peters's words. But that is real life. That is the simple, truthful way of describing how entrepreneurial companies have made their mark, survived and won. Business guru hyperbole – published and marketed and puffed until the bolts drop out – can be fun, and stimulating, but it can also be highly inappropriate, not to say irresponsible. And . . . empty. Peters describes himself as the prince of disorder, champion of bold failures, maestro of zest, professional loudmouth, corporate cheerleader and lover of markets. All great things. But we have to live too in a more real world.

It is not so much that you start off with a determination to do the one thing that takes your fancy – and, damn it, that something may have failed for everyone else but with you it will work. The process is not that. The process is that true entrepreneurs look around at what will make a difference, and select one of those differences that is within their range to attack. One could say that what corporate strategy is actually about is just that: the positioning of the company, the prioritizing of the presentation of its strengths, so that relative to its competitors it has differential, and becomes a winner. It is an intuitive process much more than a purely rational one, as we have said – what you are doing is inventing a brand by defining its characteristics. Entrepreneurs are very good at that. Big corporations are hopeless at it. Big corporations have no knack of invention. Invention, and the messianic commercialization of that invention, is what entrepreneurs do.

It's invention through self-interest, if you like, but there is pedigree in that. Jeremy Bentham, founder of the Utilitarians in the eighteenth century, argued that self-interest was the prime motive of human behaviour. 'It is not from the benevolence of the butcher, the brewer, or the baker, that we can expect our dinner, but from their regard to their own interest,' Adam Smith wrote two hundred and more years ago. Someone earning money by his own labour benefits himself, but he also – inadvertently if you will – benefits society, because to earn income from his labour in a competitive market he must produce something that others value and want. 'By directing that industry in such a manner as its produce may be of greatest value, he intends only his own gain, and he is in this, as in many other cases, led by an invisible hand to promote an end which was no part of his intention.' The main cause of prosperity, Smith argues, lies in the increasing division of labour – people of complementary and differentiated skills, driven by self-interest, working together as a team, but only doing so in the realization that the whole can achieve more than its component parts. In *The Wealth of Nations* he gives the famous example of pins. Ten workers could produce 48,000 pins a day if each of eighteen specialized tasks was assigned individually to the particular skills of particular workers. Average productivity: 4,800 pins per worker per day. But without the division of labour, and the complementary utilization of skills within a team working to a common purpose, and you have something very different. Take the same number of craftsmen, and the same number of identical tools, but this time make each worker try to do all eighteen specialized tasks for himself and by himself. He would be lucky to produce even one pin per day. Teamwork is what wins the prize, and teamwork arises through the intelligent application of self-interest.

In undeveloped economies it is difficult to challenge the self-evident truth of this. The early years of the United States would probably be the clearest example of all. On 4 July 1776, the official founding date of the US, the country was an almost empty wilderness, whose cities either did not exist at all, or were little more than coastal villages. The population of this vast land consisted of approximately half a million native Americans, who lived on the edge of starvation, and three million settlers, most of whom were semi-self-sufficient farmers living in extreme poverty. In less than two centuries the country was transformed into a continent containing 250 million of the richest people in the history of the world; a continent crisscrossed with highways, railways, telephone and telegraph lines; a continent filled with prosperous farms and dotted with innumerable towns and cities that were the sites of factories producing all manner of goods and using methods of production that probably could not even have been imagined in 1776.

How was this achieved? What Adam Smith might say, if he were able to look at the US now, was that what happened was the cumulative, aggregate result of tens of millions of people, generation after generation, each pursuing his individual self-interest, and in that process helping others to pursue their self-interests. What made this possible was individual freedom. Eastern farmers realized that the land in the mid-west and west was better for many purposes than the land in the east, and that a higher income was to be made by moving there. So they moved. Merchants realized that these farmers needed supplies and that money was to be made in supplying them. Others perceived the growing trade and the money to be made in improving transportation to the new regions. They built barge lines and stagecoach lines, then steamship companies and railroads. Businessmen and inventors, often one and the same, were constantly on the lookout for the new and the better. They discovered and introduced thousands upon thousands of improvements both in products and in methods of production, each new advance serving as the base for something still newer and still better. They built the factories and the industries that made the cities and towns. The rest of the population recognized the advantages of employment in the new industries and cities. All this happened because – I am, of course, putting words in Adam Smith's mouth – it was to the rational self-interest of individuals to make it happen and because no one could stop them from making it happen. Whether that is right or wrong, what is indisputable is that the result was by far the highest productivity per capita of any country in the world. Today, the economic glow of the United States is undoubtedly losing much of its lustre. Developed economies seem to need more sophisticated and complex remedies and dynamic forces than those in transitional growth. Developed societies need more to sustain them than undeveloped ones do. Pure self-interest, in the Adam Smith sense, is arguably no longer enough. In America's case there is no doubt as to the failure of the last two or three decades. From about 1973, productivity growth in the US took a sharp downturn and began to compound a deficit against the growth rate of most other large nations. 'Compared with the problem of slow productivity growth,' wrote Paul R. Krugman in *The Age of Diminished Expectations,* 'all other long term economic concerns – foreign competition, the industrial base, lagging technology, deteriorating infrastructure and so on – are minor issues.' The industrial heartland of the country has imploded. Entire regions – the north-east and the mid-west, once the backbone of the American economy – are in savage decline. Detroit, once the home of the American automobile industry and the leading industrial city in the world, is now on the verge of losing its last automobile factory, and growing portions of it are becoming uninhabited. The housing stock, industry and downtown shopping districts of many other large cities are also in a state of profound decay. Large-scale unemployment persists. America is not in a happy state. But once it was. One day maybe it will be again. Nothing stays still.

Nothing ever stays still for entrepreneurs, as well as for nations. You have to move and adjust the whole time. Much of the strategy detail as you move forward is simply unknowable in advance. Do not worry about that. You simply have to get into the market, try what you want to try, succeed a bit, fail a bit, and iterate towards viability and increasing success. And have the money. You have tested the strategy – it works; you have got a winner – go for it, to the limit of the funds you can sensibly raise. But in raising the money you must make sure that you surround yourself with people entirely capable of dealing with the technical functions that need to be performed. You must be wholly content to employ for these tasks people who are better than you in those respects. As Andrew Carnegie said he would like written on his gravestone: 'Here lies a man who knew how to put into his service more able men than he was himself.'

Entrepreneurial leaders carry with them a very clear sense of communication. People around them know precisely what they are trying to do. They are driven by a mission and they know how to articulate and *establish* a mission so that it becomes a cause célèbre. They have something else: the ability to say no. The pressure on leaders to do a hundred different things is overwhelming, but the best do not allow themselves to become buried – they stick to the essential issues and say no to the rest. They do not suffocate themselves, therefore. They can breathe. Too many second-raters try to do a little bit of twenty-five things and get nothing done. They are very popular because they always say yes. But they get nothing done.

Companies that survive, grow and make a pattern in the world are those that have a concept of what they can add. It is not just money, and it absolutely is not size –

it is excellence; excellence in the way that they treat their staff; excellence in the way that they search to provide real customer service; excellence in their desire to move their market on. Well – we have another swimmer against the stream in our ranks: you. You are going to create an entity that will become in time a great business. Let your business, from its earliest days, have value, in the real sense of the word. Let it have Charles Handy's 'soul'. Let it have real aspiration. Let it have happiness, and derive that happiness from the fulfilment it provides for those who spend their working lives within it.

Four

TRUST IN YOUR INTUITION

Required: Experienced Booksellers for a new bookshop – Waterstone's – in Old Brompton Road. Opening in September. The first of many. Our object is to have the best literary bookshops in the land, staffed by the best, happiest, literary booksellers.

Waterstone's recruitment advertisement

This was the recruitment advertisement I ran in London's *Evening Standard* in July 1982, eight weeks before my longed-for first branch opened. Looking at it now, it is an odd ad – though perhaps its oddness was a positive quality. Whatever – through it I recruited five experienced staff from Hatchard's in Piccadilly, at that time, and perhaps still, the most prestigious literary bookshop in England, but not one that in those days spent too much time worrying about its staff's 'happiness' (Billy Collins, the then owner, was more of the John Sainsbury/Colin Southgate school of macho management . . .). They came to me because they had been given no salary increase for three years! How lucky I was. 'Waterstone's,' purred one of my recruits into the phone, as it rang barely a second after we had opened on our first day. 'Ye gods,' I thought. 'He said "Waterstone's." "Waterstone's." It has happened. It is real. I have made it!'

That thought was more than somewhat premature, given the terrors that lay ahead, but what emerged to be a real gift to me were my Hatchard's recruits, so knowledgeable were they, so good-humoured, and so wise in the arts of charming books into customers' hands and gently extracting money from their wallets. Twenty-four years later, and they are still, in my heart, my friends. The privilege was mine. They taught me.

This actually is a great feature of life within small, ambitious start-up companies. You are a team and you learn from each other, free from big corporation career jealousies. There is no time for career jealousies. Survival is the name of the game, and when life is dangerous people stick together. They use their individual strengths and use and learn from the strengths of other members of the team. In this scenario forgiveness is very important. Inevitably, and with the best will in the world, people make mistakes. There is no time for checking and counter-checking, and people do not want that. Everyone has to learn, everyone has to forgive, and everyone has to resolve privately not to make the same mistake again. This works so well in the young, entrepreneurial company, and so badly in almost all big corporations which, for example, all too often use their appraisal systems and confidential files to record errors and misjudgements, rather than as mechanisms to identify areas of achievement and success.

Chastise people for failure, and the result is that in the future they will make it a point not to expose themselves to risk by wandering one inch off the beaten path. But corporations need to experiment, to find new ways through the jungle, to lay themselves open to the possibility of change. Chastising employees for 'failure' kills all hope of change.

I believe that the mindset that allows you to spend your working life thanking and congratulating people rather than being unpleasant to them is a mainstay of good leadership. I like much of what Carly Fiorina did and said when she was chief executive of Hewlett-Packard, frantic as her wafty rhetoric drove her fellow directors, we learnt on her eventual dismissal. There is elegance in her often-stated theme that by rewarding the good in people who work for you, and forgiving or ignoring the bad in them, in time you will succeed in driving out that bad. Good schoolteachers could have told us all that aeons ago, of course. A less than good teacher will allocate praise and blame equally, except that, tragically, all the praise will be for academic work, and all the blame for behaviour. Good teachers know that if you give only praise for both academic work and behaviour equally, then it works. Stop criticizing – praise. Praise wins. By means of praise you get both – good work and good behaviour.

Give your new company a character whereby good performance and good conduct are the subject of sincere, open approval and congratulation, and reduce criticism of underperformance to the very minimum. It is a very pleasant way of conducting one's affairs. But there is an interesting conundrum that underlies this. It is my suspicion that a great majority of entrepreneurs, and perhaps the most successful of them, are driven in part by an inability to forgive themselves. They can forgive others – are perhaps quite exemplary in their willingness to do that as they work with their team – but cannot forgive themselves. There will be some aspect of their past that haunts them and drives them to expunge the memory of it by the overt public demonstration that they are brave, risk-taking entrepreneurs.

To be frank, this was exactly the case with me. There were aspects of my history and my personality that I hated myself for, not least the (perhaps deserved?) contempt shown to me by my late father, and I needed Waterstone's – why do you think it was named after me? – to be a public demonstration of quality and worth and standing. I would have died for Waterstone's – literally, died for it. There is no real courage in a drunk Russian soldier, weapons exhausted, standing to hurl bottles at a German tank. He is drunk. He is without fear. There *is* real courage, however, in a terrified young man, bowels churning in fear, not an ounce of aggression in him, pushing himself up one more time to climb the trench wall. I was the former – the drunk Russian soldier – hurling bottles at my past which I could not forgive, drunk with the exhilaration of having the opportunity of restating my personal worth and standing through Waterstone's high-profile success. That is just a little insane. And an insane, bottle-hurling foe is tough for the corporate opponent to measure up to.

There is one person who will prove to be precious to you, if a bottle thrower you are: and that is someone – your spouse, a sibling, an old colleague – who is capable of moderating some of the rougher edges of your passion and conduct as you drive your dream forward. You could do with a friendship close enough, frank enough, to help you in this. I particularly say this as a close Indian friend reminded me recently that there is a lovely concept of friendship within the Buddhist tradition: the 'noble friend', or *kalyanamitra*, someone who is so close to you that any attempt by you at pretension is ignored, and you will be gently confronted with your own area of 'blindness'. We all of us carry a blind spot – literally – in the retinas of our eyes. The Buddhist believes that there is, equally, a blind spot in your soul, and that you depend on the *kalyanamitra* to see for you where you cannot see yourself.

You need not go so far as to become a Buddhist (though you would have my admiration if you did), but, if you can, have someone like that for you. Somebody to watch over you uncritically and creatively to moderate the rougher edges of your conduct and your drive as you and your company move on your way. There is a mountain of stress awaiting you. You can deal with that, because that is the sort of person you are. But accept help, when good help is there for you. It may prove precious as you face up to the terrifying problems and challenges that certainly await you.

One point about that mountain of stress ahead of you incidentally (and I deliver it from the heart): as your company drives forward there will be occasions when you come up against an apparent brick wall, leaving you with nowhere to go. The technique when this happens is to stay still for a little, and wait for movement. The tectonic plates are always shifting, and after a time a chink will appear, a shaft of light maybe where you were least expecting it, and you will find your way around, through or over that wall, and resume your drive forward. Carl Jung tells us that in the last analysis there is no such thing as an insoluble problem, and that if you can raise yourself to it you will simply outgrow it; others, however, unable to raise themselves, will allow that problem to destroy them. What Jung means, I think, is that you can train yourself to move 'above' the problem, shifting your perspective to a wider horizon, so that what appeared to be insoluble simply loses its urgency and uniqueness. Jung says:

> What, on a lower level, had led to the wildest conflicts and to emotions full of panic, viewed from a higher level of the personality, now seemed like a storm in the valley seen from a high mountain top. This does not mean that the thunderstorm is robbed of its reality; it means that, instead of being in it, one is now above it.

By moving above and away from the problem you avoid the rawest edges of personal stress. You reattach yourself to the motivating force that is driving you and you move on. Money is of course one of those motivating forces, and a prime one. To deny that would be absurd. But, as we have said, the desire to be seen as a public success is sometimes the most compulsive element of all. There is an endemic insecurity among entrepreneurs, even the greatest of them. As Patience Wheatcroft of *The Times* once said, Philip Green, for example, might accept, in his quieter moments, that his quite extraordinary coup with Bhs – bought out of public ownership for a song, and barely two years later valued at billions – probably gave him more pleasure for the message it sent to his City critics than for the money it heaped on his already vast private wealth. He had been so badly bruised by the Amber Day debacle in the early nineties, when he lost his job effectively on the back of just a single missed profit target, and the pain of that seemed still to be nagging at him. He bathed in his Bhs triumph, as well he might, and yet the degree of his desire for public acclaim became risible. Private company it might now be under his ownership, but his results were given a publicity launch, wholly superfluous in a private company, that might have looked excessive for the brashest big public corporation, reminiscent of the high days of Tiny Rowland and Lonrho.

Gerald Ronson's brave and successful efforts to bring his Heron Group, once Britain's second largest private company, back to centre stage after his prison sentence for his involvement in the Guinness affair should have been sufficient private joy unto himself. And yet it somehow was not, quite extraordinary achievement though it was. The flamboyant charitable work, the rather forced attempts to be seen all the time with the great and the good – he seems to require continual reassurance of his public standing, to the extent that the insecurity underlying his personality lies uncomfortably exposed.

There may be something of the same in Sir Peter Davis. He was a doomed man in many eyes when his conceit – or nagging sense of personal inadequacy? – allowed him, when chairman of Prudential, to front a particularly embarrassing series of television commercials. Embarrassing, that is, to those who like Peter Davis, and knew he was making a fool of himself. To the outside world this was a personal vanity too far, and perhaps the first mark of suspicion against him before he went off to Sainsbury's – disastrously – as their chief executive. Rather similar were the portraits of Sir Jack Cohen in his heyday at Tesco, what seemed to be dozens of them, in the foyer and up and down the stairs; the vast pink and pastel picture of Colin Southgate in the EMI boardroom; the bronze bust of the insufferable, strutting little Lord Stevens of Ludgate that used to sit in the middle of the entrance hall of Express Newspapers, removed subsequently to some distant cellar when Clive Hollick took the group over.

Peter Simon, a former nudist hippy, the prodigiously rich and successful founder of Monsoon, one of the UK's leading clothing chains, is of a different cut to this, and I admire him. He may have started off his business on a barrow on London's Portobello Road, but it was on Beauchamp Place in Knightsbridge that his first shop appeared in 1973. Monsoon succeeded because the quality of Simon's product was of such a high standard, though always sensibly priced. He cared about profit – of course – but most of all he cared about the quality of his product, and indeed the quality of his life. His headquarters, by no means extravagant, carry a statement of that in his fine display of contemporary and Third World art, and he is an inspirational owner of the wonderful Electric Cinema in London's Notting Hill. I admire entrepreneurs who, like Peter Simon, support the arts because they recognize that art feeds the soul, rather than because they want the social cachet for doing so (and boy, have I sat on committees where the trustees are so clearly there for just that . . .). I once scribbled down a comment by the journalist Libby Purves, I think shortly after she interviewed me for *The Times*. I thought she had it just right, and unpretentiously so. I have lost the note but I remember I hope the sense of it – she was saying that art works as only art can, in the way that it enlightens life and fosters humanity. And this is not necessarily art at its most grandiloquent but in its tangential moments: a fragment of a poem suddenly brought to mind; a Baltic landscape in a gallery window; the pool of stage lighting on a dancer's shoulders, recalling the first Caravaggio figure one ever saw; a two- or three-bar phrase from Elgar's *Gerontius*. One glimpses again suddenly, sharply, the fragility of human life, and the beauty of it, and its inexplicable sense of truth.

Which brings me to say this: one golden rule to have in mind in the launch of any new entrepreneurial consumer business in Britain today is that we are a nation that is generally culturally trading up – and emphatically so – rather than dumbing down. The received wisdom for most of my adult life was that the trend was the reverse of this; that our culture was inexorably coarsening, and that society – all of it – was hell bent on the route to trivia and philistinism. Nothing could be further from the case, the way things are going now. Maybe it never was true, and the received wisdom, as usual, plain wrong. In 2004, more people went to a museum or an art gallery than to a live sporting event or a theme park. The radio station Classic FM has been one of the most commercially successful broadcasting initiatives ever, anywhere. Put on a big show at one of London's museums – Caravaggio at the National Gallery, Matisse at the Royal Academy – and your paying audience might well exceed half a million people, they will have booked weeks ahead, and travelled from all over the country to get there. Tate Modern is crowded every day of the year. The Royal Festival Hall, one of the biggest concert halls in the world, is customarily packed to the roof for the London Philharmonic or the Philharmonia.

This is by no means simply a London phenomenon either. Aided they may have been by free entry, but visitors to Liverpool's big museums have doubled in recent years, and Manchester's Museum of Science and Industry by over 50 per cent. In Gateshead we have the new Baltic art gallery, a source of great civic pride for its quite stunning architecture. The Symphony Hall in Birmingham, the Bridgewater Hall in Manchester, both wonderful buildings packed to the rafters night after night, run by people who these days could not be more aware of their civic duty to reach out into the communities and attract and hold the biggest audiences they can muster. I do not care if 'outreach' is a gratingly politically correct term. In these centres of cultural excellence outreach is now genuinely being made to work. And the fact that it is working helps make my point that the entrepreneur can with perfect confidence aim right into a culturally traded-up market sector. (That is just the way to attack the big corporates, who invariably get themselves trapped in the middle market.) A MORI survey in 1999 indicated that about 45 per cent of people felt that there was nothing in museums that they wanted to see. Just five years later barely 19 per cent told MORI they felt that. This could hardly be more encouraging.

We are a good society, and we are getting even better. A good society appreciates that knowledge, education, history and the arts actually matter. And as that culture grows, so does the happiness and sense of completeness of the people. And so do the peculiarly satisfying trading opportunities for entrepreneurs to build their brands.

Peter Simon's dream was about selling very good clothes of a certain rather idiosyncratic style, at an affordable price in stylish, quirky stores. He wanted to make money out of that – but first, he wanted to brand the high street with the Monsoon name. There was beauty for him in the Monsoon name and concept. For another entrepreneur, the dream might be to produce the most beautiful ceramics. Monsoon's lovely clothes, another man's ceramics – the purpose of the great entrepreneurial companies has, almost always, an aspirational ring to it. Profit, in time, will be a result of that, but that is what it is – a result, a stated necessity, but not in itself a purpose. Those profits, reinvested, allow the company to do more and more and push the dream yet further.

So what happened to Peter Simon? He took Monsoon off the main stock market and placed it on the secondary Alternative Investment Market en route to taking it private once more. He did so because he found he was not prepared to proceed either with the short-termism of quarterly reporting, or the need to boost dividends endlessly. What he wanted to

do with the money was reinvest it in Monsoon's product quality and its international expansion, rather than fill the pockets
of speculative third-party investors. They were not part of the
dream he had shared and nurtured with his team, his staff.

Peter Simon, as I have said, is now a man of gargantuan
wealth, but if you start out with the purpose of simply making
money you can very easily make a colossal ass of yourself. It
looks a little like that, for example, with Terry Green, whose
search via Allders for a way to get his name up there with his
friend and former colleague Philip Green has the appearance,
as Patience Wheatcroft has written, of more than anything
else a desire to become as rich as his mentor. Philip Green is
a genuinely brilliant, creative retailer, and a devil for the operational detail. Of course he has entrepreneurial guts and drive
– by the bucket-load – but there is much more to him than
zeal. Or greed. He is extremely creative, but also extremely
diligent, having an eagle eye for how costs can be reduced
and margins grown without damaging product quality, store
presentation or operational efficiencies. Terry Green, in contrast, did not appear to display, in his brief Allders experience,
a flare for either creativity or operational diligence. It was a
high-profile buy for him but he failed to demonstrate to
observers any very clear idea of what he wanted to do with
it. The press coverage he received on Allders' demise, with
staff, pensioners and creditors left badly exposed, must have
hurt him a great deal.

Back to Green, Philip, for a moment, whom, notwith-
standing Amber Day, many would consider not just a brilliant

retail entrepreneur, but an extraordinary corporate strategist as well. Professor Kenichi Ohmae, described by the *Financial Times* as 'Japan's only successful management guru', defined corporate strategy as a discipline that aims to alter the company's strength relative to that of its competitors. That is fair enough, the more so if one accepts my central thesis that the process is as much about insight and intuition as rationality. It is not so much plodding rationalism as invention and flair that win the day – and that is where strategic planning within big corporates can so clearly fall down. Big corporations tend to have forgotten how to invent. Flair – inventiveness – looks like danger. But both are crucial. Even within mammoth businesses like Bhs and Arcadia, Philip Green has that capacity to embrace invention and flair, align both of these to operational tightness, and emerge with a 'product' that most successfully commercializes the inventive flair from which it originated.

But even now in his fully evolved, mature version, he is probably a performer much better suited to operating within the private rather than public markets. Private, you have the space and time to get out there, try a few things, fail a few times, and test yourself towards effective solutions; and then give those solutions every ounce of financial investment you can muster to drive them on to quantum scale. In the public market you have Wall Street or City of London short-termism – every quarter up and up – to balance against long-term strategy and long-term viability. Incidentally, City short-termism could be blamed on hedge funds, as is the current fashion, on the basis that they distort capital and commodity markets in the interests of making fast bucks; but conventional institutional investors do much the same thing, if under a rather more polite guise. In the latter case they have the actuaries at their backs, rather than greedy individuals, but it all adds up to much the same. In addition it is worth reflecting that the modern received wisdom of allocating shares to public company executives in order to align their interests with the shareholders perhaps too successfully does precisely that. Public company shareholders, gamblers to a man, want quick wins. The company – the true company – might best be served by wins down the line, perhaps a decade or more down the line, rather than now. With their interests aligned, however, the public company chief executives (average tenure of office currently less than four years in a recent survey!), the institutional investors and the hedge funds, all in unison, have no truck with nonsense like that.

I mentioned Kodak earlier – let me use them as an example once again. Kodak saw digital photography emerge through the market ether and, sensibly, tried to get behind it. They invested, and profitably grew their digital photography division to over a billion dollars. But not profitably enough for Wall Street, who wanted more, quarterly, and reliably so, without a single hitch. Well, there was a hitch or two – how could there not have been in an experimental technology? – and Kodak were forced to put their new division on the backburner. Smooth progression in Kodak's quarterly results resumed, and Wall Street, having proved itself inadequate to deal with the opportunity that the new digital photography provided, smiled contentedly. This is an example where the venture capitalists, the private equity players, can and do have a real role, by taking public companies private allowing them, outside public gaze, just a little space and time to experiment and evolve. The public company Kodak, with unrivalled expertise in this market, was too cramped by the short-term stock valuation aspirations of the secondary market shareholders to be allowed the elbow room it needed to make a real success of it.

It really is a tightrope for public corporations. Wall Street or the City of London do not like slips or experimentation, but experimentation is the stuff of life. Even the mighty Proctor & Gamble is said to have settled on the fact that it will have a new product failure rate of over 85 per cent. And this from one of the most painstaking and supposedly sophisticated market research organizations in the world. It launches one hundred new products into the market, having market-researched that demographic segment to the point of death, and only fifteen of those products survive. That is not a strike rate that will help the share price.

There is another point here. Just why is it that only fifteen out of a hundred new products work (and we can move away from P&G in the certain knowledge that for other big consumer product corporations the ratio is probably even worse)? Well, obviously they failed because they turned out to be the wrong products. Why were they the wrong products? Because they never represented a real need. They were artificial creations arising from an over-rational source – demographic segmentation. I think the problem with over-rational, under-intuitive research work of this type – I did this stuff for my living when I was twenty-five or twenty-six years old – is that none of us in real life actually acts according to one single demographic or attitudinal category. We are all of us complex and pluralistic beyond measure. Let's just keep it obvious by applying a simple example. Waterstone's was aimed at me. I knew that I wanted, and badly needed in my life, bookshops just like the ones I was creating. I simply assumed that plenty of other people, no doubt all of wildly differing demographics, would find once they saw them that they wanted them too. Well – they did.

Years later, however, a new marketing director explained to me that we were missing millions in potential sales, because his market research was showing that only 20 per cent of the public felt comfortable with the Waterstone's offer. We had to change it, he said – popularize it, 'push the envelope' – and urgently. Eighty per cent of the nation's adults felt positively uncomfortable with it – we were too literary, too wide a choice, too higher education, too intellectual. I told him to look at his research again. Twenty per cent of the adult population loved the stores, and for exactly those reasons. What is more, they were buying from us on average at least fifty books a year each. Some, double that figure. We would change not one jot. Let the 80 per cent go to WHSmith instead.

John Beale did the same a few years earlier with his Early

Learning Centre stores and mail order toy business. ELC was tightly focused, quite uniquely, at educationally responsible and aspirational parents of very young children (my colleagues and I were fortunate enough to buy ELC in April 2004). What we were both doing at the same time in our separate markets was satisfying a real, actual need: not the theoretical demand of market research or demographic segmentation, but actual demand.

Both Waterstone's and ELC were bound to work. My Daisy & Tom stores too. Eighty-five out of one hundred Proctor & Gamble products, however, clearly satisfy no real need at all. They will be artificial constructs, created out of an excess of predictability being placed on theories of demographic segmentation that in fact carry no predictability whatsoever. None. Just volatility. In reality consumers behave, in everything they do in relationship to everything else, entirely unpredictably. As the media commentator John Gilder has said, where people are most obviously similar is in their prurient interests. Everyone has sex and shopping in common. Where people most clearly differentiate themselves is in their civilized interests. But in none of these interests, prurient or civilized, are we in any degree stereotyped. None of us. We use Colgate toothpaste only because it reminds us of our mother. Who could have predicted that? We have an aversion to the colour grey because our bullying father wore nothing else. Predictable? We like brandy, but we do not like gin. It really is true – our buying across brands and products is in practice wildly too diverse to make up into a pattern. Asinine market research questionnaires show the desperation of the professionals here: 'Do you prefer traditional goods or contemporary goods?' I was asked by a researcher on a London high street recently. She looked a sweet kid, but my heart dropped as I glanced at the questions on her clipboard and saw that there was at least ten minutes of this drivel to go.

It is intuition that works. Just intuition. Philip Green, as long as he owns them, will, by his intuition, evolve Bhs and Arcadia into ever-improved versions of the original model. He will have to, because he knows that there is always a new generation of fresh-thinking, highly ambitious newcomers on their way to liven things up for him. You have to watch, watch, watch. Never underrate the newcomer with the interesting, fresh idea. Big corporations do that at their peril – but they still do it. The newcomer's balance sheet may be a joke, but it could be they are on to something really good; so good that given time they will knock the big corporation into serious disarray. Don't look at the newcomer's accounts. Just watch the customers coming through their doors. Remember EasyJet's arrival in the market?

It is an odd thing that established corporations – US, UK, wherever – have such trouble in either countering or embracing what Professor Clayton Christensen – who before going into academia at Harvard Business School worked as an assistant to two US transportation secretaries during the Reagan years – would call the 'disruptive' innovations that are on their radar screens. The problem for the big corporates seems to be that they develop mindsets and processes that revolve around one thing: what they already know. Once that pattern has become embedded their managers find it difficult, even career threatening, to justify to others or even to themselves the need to turn their processes upside down to respond to the disruptive newcomers. Make too much fuss and you appear, in corporate speak, to be 'excitable' and 'unsound', and your career card marked accordingly. The big corporations relish and support a managerial mindset that revolves around what the corporation already does. They want, at all costs, to keep life stable and predictable.

But leave it too late, and the entrepreneurial newcomer has made his play, got his position and seized his lead. And by seizing the lead, he has secured for himself a gold-strewn exit by trade sale to the market leader should he wish to go down that route, when he can cash in and start-up another business. Exit valuations based on purely financial perform-ance measurements – cash generation multiples, or balance sheet net worth – won't matter if he plays his cards right. He will get almost any price he wants, so that the corporate can bury the embarrassment and get him and his upstart business off their screens.

It can certainly be tough for big corporations trying to hold their position when all about them is newcomer inno-vation and change. Take Dell, run by some of the cleverest, smartest people any of us could imagine. They arrived on the scene at the lowest end, one might say – but captured that market and manipulated it quite brilliantly. Their little

PCs, with all their off-the-shelf components, created havoc with the seamless progression of Digital. Then Dell moved onwards and upwards from offering just personal computers to servers and work stations. But the current wave in the market is for handheld, wireless computing and communications. Dell's great strengths have been in outsourcing and logistics capabilities, and in custom configuring devices to the specifications of individual customers. Those are not the processes required to design and manufacture the handheld devices of the new market wave. Suddenly, the tables have turned. Dell has become the clumsy corporate.

Competitive strategy (which was the title of Michael Porter's seminal 1980 book) can perhaps lead to excessive focus on competitive advantage. This, in turn, leads companies to think too narrowly about their strategic options. The net result is that industries converge on a single paradigm. The strikingly similar business models of the large airlines are one clear example of this 'convergent' thinking. The danger is that companies become blinded to opportunities for fundamental innovation in the way customers are served. And so the likes of JetBlue and People Express, which dared to think outside the airline paradigm, continue to suck value away from the big carriers. So, forget your competitors for a moment. Ask, instead, questions such as: what factors can we eliminate that the industry has taken for granted?

The markets within which the corporates operate are not easy for them, such is the pace of divergence and change. You think you know the market, but you never do. A conventional challenge from a conventional competitor is one thing – with a steady nerve, and a deep enough wallet, that challenge can be contained. But the unconventional entrant, whose technology or thesis may seem barmy when first seen, may cause you complete havoc. Think Charles Schwab, or then e-Trade, and their discount brokerages, encouraging a whole new wave of day traders. Think online spread-betting on share prices, and the conventional stock markets.

The orthodox rules of big corporate life, as learnt on every MBA induction course, do not apply when the rogue player arrives on the scene. The orthodox rules – skilful planning, strong customer focus, diligent execution according to a Plan – are all very sound. In existing, steady-state businesses, orthodoxy can be great – if stiff and ultra left-brain – but in today's technology world you do not have the time, as, monthly almost, new markets emerge for new technologies. Maybe you should not have the time, for absolutely everyone (independent 'experts', the corporations) has a consistently dismal record in forecasting demand, and how large these emerging markets will prove to be. One can be certain that the new technology will be a catalyst for explosive growth in some area or another, probably in one that its progenitors have not yet perceived. Identifying those authentic new markets accurately, and then commercially exploiting them, is crucial if Dell, Hewlett-Packard and the rest of them are to enjoy the continued growth well into the future on which their shareholders are speculating, and, incomparably more importantly, on which their staff depend.

It is not backroom research that will identify new markets for you; it is people. Too much emphasis on strategy and you will simply get stuck. There is a balance to strive for here. As Tom Peters would say, put extraordinary people around you and you will never get stuck. Extraordinary people will find the extraordinary innovative product and provide the extraordinary customer experience – and that is all you need. Extraordinary people will also have the knack, with you, of setting limits and defining goals; that is what the essence of strategy is, in my mind. Weak managers try to do too much. And the weak big corporates tend to do not much more than ape their competitors, which is the mindset they have, the safety play, but which in the long run will never work.

In the short term the big corporates can fight away on price, and better operational effectiveness; that is playing to their strengths. They can bully suppliers, and they have the leverage of a big infrastructure. But these are no more than short-term ploys. Eventually you have to stand apart. You have to be unique – and identifying and displaying uniqueness, differential, is what entrepreneurs are good at. More than that, the entrepreneur's genius lies in looking at the company, looking at their product, and picking out what there is within it that can be delivered as a proposition. A *promise*. Your brand – for me Waterstone's, my lovely Daisy & Tom children's stores, now Early Learning Centre too – is your promise. The product you sell is in itself not wholly significant. What makes it significant is the brand that covers it – and the brand is the promise of something worthwhile, dependable and identified to your cultural and ethical standard and model. This is an intuitive and personal art. Entrepreneurs are much better at it than the corporates. Corporates buy up entrepreneurial innovations, then coarsen and ruin them. They never seem to understand the brands they have bought, and the promise that they deliver. You have to stand apart. You have to be unique.

This is especially true today, when the flow of information and capital is incredibly fast, and available to all. The entrepreneur can be as well served by information access and capital as his corporate opponent. No clear advantage to the corporates there, then. Indeed, they may actually find themselves to be disadvantaged. Typically, they remain blocked and fettered by the low productivity of their lower and middle managers, whom they probably have in their thousands. Their productivity is low because their utilization is low.

Until quite recently it was a mark of pride for companies to do everything in house. That was the mark of a serious corporation. Now, we have all discovered outsourcing – but most look on outsourcing as a way of cutting costs, which I believe is the case, but not wholly the point. What outsourcing does is vastly to improve the quality of the people who still work for you. The golden rule is this: you should outsource everything for which there is no career track that could lead into senior management. When you outsource to a total quality control expert he is busy forty-eight weeks a year working for you and a number of other clients on something he sees as challenging, whereas a person in that role employed within the company is busy six weeks a year and the rest of the time is writing memoranda. And looking for something to do. And playing office politics.

Outsourcing can lead you to much more effectiveness. Outsourcing the management of information technology, data processing and computer systems has become quite routine, even in the most traditional companies. By the early 1990s most American computer firms had outsourced the production of their hardware to manufacturers in Japan or Singapore – unthinkable a decade before. By the late 1990s practically every Japanese consumer-electronics company had decided to play the ball back, and the manufacturing of its products for at least the American market had been outsourced to American contract manufacturers.

Human Resources (again – has there ever been a colder, more insulting term?), or Personnel as they used to call themselves, is a particularly interesting example of what an entrepreneurial company may instinctively wish to place outside these days; more so than the corporates, who would truly regard personnel functions as part of their traditional life blood. A recent McKinsey study stated that the human resources management of more than two million American workers – their hiring and firing, their training, the settlement of their benefits packages and the rest of it – has been out-sourced to professional employee organizations. The trend is developing very fast from virtually a nil base ten years or so ago, and what is interesting is that whereas at first the inroads were within small and medium-sized companies, now the biggest of the consulting firms manage employment issues for a number of *Fortune* 500 companies (including BP).

McKinsey calculate that outsourcing human relations management can save up to 30 per cent of the cost, but, as I have said above, to me that is not the whole point of it. You get, or should get, the cost savings, and that is very good, but you also put your HR function in the hands of total experts in their narrow, specialist field, who do absolutely nothing else, and therefore do it very well (though in no circumstances would I personally let them get anywhere near the hiring and firing functions, as I have said earlier). The same principle applies I think to all outsourcing options – in small and medium early-stage entrepreneurial companies it is often nearly impossible to recruit top expertise in some of the back-office functions. Yes, you can find and motivate and give wonderful jobs to the product people, the merchants, the merchandisers and the marketing folk, but some of the back-office functions – finance, HR, property – are often really difficult to recruit into, as these people are less easily motivated and excited by the entrepreneurial vision. The result of that is you can end up finding yourself employing the second and third best – disastrously, and probably more expensively than outsourcing the function to external experts.

The entrepreneur is an instinctive outsourcer, predominantly because he has a horror of burdensome bureaucracy. Some of the most successful entrepreneur companies you can find will have specific (rather than general) expertise, simple forms and absolutely minimal HQ staff, which provides them with a real point of advantage against the corporates in terms of bustle and drive. I like what McGill University's Professor Henry Mintzberg teaches about the connection, or more frequently disconnection, between big corporate senior management and their underlying operation. He says that the problem lies in the inaccuracies of management education, and the business school practice of training people about management in general, totally out of the context of their own organizations. They are given the impression that what you do is sit there at the head of the hierarchy and make great decisions. Harvard emphasizes that it trains decision makers, facilitators, builders of culture, the headstones of the present-day cult of management. But you cannot teach swimming by reading about it. The problem with so many of the big corporations is that people – leaders – are parachuted in who do not really know a lot about the businesses they are being hired to run. In real life, in the non-corporate world where the good guys live, no one would dream of risking their family's last penny opening a restaurant without being absolutely sure they knew how to do it. 'General management skills' does not mean a thing in this context. Nor does 'strategic vision'. This is real life.

The business of parachuting in general managers as leaders does not work and does not deserve to work. It can lead to real disaster, and a totally disaffected company. And disaffection, if it is allowed to fester, can lead all too soon, and astonishingly quickly, to the spiral of coarsening and decline of the company that once held such creative entrepreneurial brilliance, and uniqueness, and was such a source of happiness and pride to those who worked there.

To suggest that such a fate might eventually befall the company you yourself founded is very tough to contemplate. It is, though, a real risk, as new management starts to come in, maybe recruited by someone else and maybe quite wrong for the task. So I think the truth is this: the real long-term win you have to hope for for your creation is longevity. I think it is no more and no less than surviving. Everybody sees crisis in their lives, momentary or prolonged, and every company does too. It is not the fact that an individual makes mistakes that is significant: what is significant is how he or she deals with those mistakes. Companies too. Individuals who face up to their mistakes, and by facing up to them conquer them, are winners in life. They survive. Companies also, in exactly the same way. You survive because you face up to mistakes, and you face up to changes in your market or your environment that threaten you.

But corporate survival over the long term is not at all easy. Here is a most interesting statistic, and it is by no means an encouraging one for the big corporates. Have a look at the *Fortune* list of the hundred biggest companies at the beginning of the twenty-first century. Compare that with the list at the beginning of the twentieth century. There is only one – *one* – company common to both lists: General Electric. It might be true that with roughly half of GE's revenues now arising from their activities in financial services the company is very different from the one Thomas Edison founded, but, for all that, GE has survived. None of its ninety-nine peers on the hundred-strong list has. We must stress that their constituent parts and divisions (entrepreneurial start-ups probably, in their time) may have survived, may have thrived indeed, under different ownership, but the overarching corporations themselves have not. There was something there in the GE culture – something there in the culture of all the decades-old survivors you can find anywhere – that has given General Electric the wisdom, flexibility and imagination to move, adjust and adapt to the times, without losing the heart of its identity. I think we are back to Charles Handy's concept of corporate soul.

Another way of looking at it is this. You could say that a company starts out in a direction conceived by the founder, and in nine out of ten of companies that end up being successful, they realized that the detail of the original strategy, the small print, did not entirely work. By means of continual and thorough experimentation and trial and error in the market, the successful company, under the entrepreneur, happens upon or iterates towards a strategy and a business model that really is viable, and, subject to a continuing process of adjustment to the market, will remain so. The changes may be very small – imperceptible even, to the outside eye – but they are made.

By 'adjustment to the market' I am not talking about self-doubt or dwindling self-assurance. Far from it. I am talking about the reverse of that. I am talking about huge self-assurance, the knowledge that it is you that will stay ahead of the pack. Like salmon, there are dozens of you swimming upstream, but because you are the smartest, the most adaptable, the most determined and the most wholly self-confident, you and your team know that it will be you who emerges as the winner. The win will not be in entirely your original form, because you and your successors will have adjusted and flexed.

Nokia are the best example of all this, starting life in the latter part of the nineteenth century as a paper mill on the banks of the river Nokia in southern Finland. There was something in the company's mindset that had pure genius within it. Nokia didn't simply adapt – they embraced change, with unshakable self-confidence. They set out to conquer the world. By buying Finnish Cable Works a little after the Second World War they entered the telephone cable market. It was their experience within that that gave them their entrée to the world of mobile phones. Heaven knows what their next move will be. Nokia changes shape because the world changes shape around them, but the original creation, the spirit of the company, will still be there, because the heart of that creation contained strengths that had staying power, were worthwhile and were solid.

And you – the founding entrepreneur – will know something of great personal worth: your personality, even many years after you have gone, will be thought of as having become embedded in the culture of the company. Succeeding generations of managers and owners may try to pretend otherwise and eradicate it, but it will never really work. Your influence will survive for a very long time. For what you will have done, once your creation has grown to the point where it has real life and survival potential, is transfer your beliefs, values and basic assumptions to the mental models of your staff. This process of building and embedding the company's culture occurs because, typically, the entrepreneur only hires and keeps people who think and feel like he or she does. It also happens because a good entrepreneur, a real entrepreneur, acts as a role model. If they are accepted and followed, their beliefs, their values and assumptions are internalized within the staff, and internalized, irremovably, within the company's culture. The influence of the first John Sainsbury is still there in Sainsbury's, still treated as a marker. Terence Conran's too, at Habitat, and most benignly John Beale's at Early Learning Centre.

Sometimes the legacy has a certain irony to it. If the leader had, for example, conflicts between on the one hand wanting to maintain complete control and on the other wanting to reward subordinates for individual prowess in solving problems, then we may see embedded in the company's culture a certain inconsistency in policies around decision making, incentives and rewards. One might say, therefore, that for better or worse the legacy of the founding entrepreneur is typically a certain structural neurosis in the organization: a pattern of living in which there are various degrees of conflict, and uneven areas of strength and weaknesses. It is interesting to observe. Once the conflicts become embedded they cannot easily be changed, because they will also have become associated with a prior history of success – the glory days of struggle, the Long March, and then, at last, victory – and are therefore taken for granted as being the best and natural way, for that organization, of doing things.

This whole transitional period from being a bold entrepreneurial newcomer to a more conventional fully established company is not at all easy. One factor is that in the interim you will have attracted imitators (for example Ottakar's copying Waterstone's, or Southwest Airlines and People Express), who themselves have become successful to at least some degree. The market within which you have been operating will have matured and changed – perhaps greatly, perhaps subtly. Products too. And the intense, neurotic drive of your company in its early days will have had to adapt to a shifting market, new, perhaps severe competition, your own increasing size and complexity, and the fact that you and your team are growing older and, perhaps, more tired.

It is at this moment that trouble can strike – and I saw that in Waterstone's. Actually, it is not so much the sudden striking of disaster, but rather the early signs of a falter. The conventional wisdom, I suppose, is that what was so powerful in the young company – the messianic drive, the compulsive vision, the super-high energy, the ability to absorb extreme stress – may serve to become, in time, a liability. This is the moment to stabilize, conventional wisdom will say, to search for higher efficiencies, to deal with the commodification of the company's products, and to evolve or bring in from the outside world a new generation of leaders for what will necessarily now be a different kind of future.

Conventional wisdom may be right in some instances – though in my view not many – but what will be absolutely certain is that the founding entrepreneur will find it extremely difficult to let go. For extremely difficult, read emotionally entirely incapable. Big corporates will point to their entrepreneurial competitors and say that what you never get in these companies is proper management development, with succession typically based on criteria that are not so much irrelevant as wrong. For example, they would say that the people who get promoted are the ones whose working style most closely resembles that of the entrepreneur, and the only people who succeed in catching the entrepreneur's eye are those who have specific skills within the market in which the company is operating. (In Waterstone's case, no doubt my enemies would have said that I was only interested in promoting people of literary interests, whether or not they had any general management skills. I rather think they might have been right. And I rather think that I was right as well. Because that was precisely why Waterstone's was Waterstone's.) The caricature is that founding entrepreneurs are only interested in, and only respect, staff within the emotionally satisfying 'creative' functions of product and sales and marketing, and demean the orthodox, rational, general 'managerial' functions such as human resources (*particularly* human resources), finance and planning. Right-brainers and left-brainers again.

Whatever. What is certainly true is that this moment when the entrepreneur starts to prepare to release power can be a truly cataclysmic time. All can be lost. An unsuccessful leader at this stage is one who will prevent potential successors from having the kind and quality of learning experiences that would enable them to take over. And, worse still, act to undermine them. Successful leaders at this stage are the ones who either have enough personal insight to adjust and broaden with the organization, or ones who recognize their own limitations and parameters and permit other forms of leadership to emerge. If neither of these processes occurs, the organization often finds itself having to develop other power centres such as boards and political cabals who force the founder out of the chief executive role into other roles, or out of the organization altogether. A new chief executive then comes in with the mandate to help the organization grow and remain successful. Very difficult to do. It seldom if ever works. The departure of the founder in these circumstances will invariably leave the rawest wounds. See the Steve Jobs example in this book's final paragraphs.

The other situation is that the entrepreneur decides to sell, does so, leaves, and then finds it too difficult to trust the new owners – almost always for very good reason – properly to protect and develop the asset they have acquired. There is an undoubted phenomenon around this: those who sell often want to buy it back quickly. Charlie Smallbone, of Small-bone of Devizes, the upmarket kitchen designer, is a good example. Smallbone was bought in 1988 by the industrial conglomerate Williams Holdings for £36 million against £4 million profits. Charlie Smallbone, head of the family firm, probably meant to stay, but in the event left almost immediately, and Williams Holdings, unperturbed, were content that they would run Smallbone themselves, and would do so far more commercially successfully under their 'professionals' than the sleepy old family owners. In the event, Williams had no idea, of course, how to do it. They starved the business of cash, they saw collapse on their hands and, I would like to think blushing, sold it back to Charlie Smallbone in 2003 for barely a quarter of what they had paid for it. It took Charlie Smallbone just a matter of weeks to turn the ship around, and put it on the stock market, where it is now thriving. Take Virgin too. Virgin went into public ownership in the 1980s, but Richard Branson hated the experience, and took the company private again. Andrew Lloyd Webber did exactly the same with The Really Useful Group. The estate agency Chestertons, fashion retailers Ted Baker – there are many examples out there of people who have sold their company, bought it back, then sold it again and bought it back again. Watch what happens now with Mr Stelios and EasyJet.

Why does this happen? It is partly for the money of course, for there is no doubt that much money can be made in rescuing firms, at commensurately low prices, from the buffoonish antics of inappropriate corporate or private equity owners. And it is not difficult; the founding entrepreneur can restore the company to its proper fortunes with sometimes extraordinary speed and ease, recreating its founding culture, stripping out centralization and its attendant bureaucratic layers, replacing muddle with clarity of purpose. Sometimes there is a recidivist flavour to it all. Nowhere more so than in Kirk Kerkorian, who has bought and sold MGM no fewer than three times, each time making huge sums of money for himself, as first Ted Turner bought then sold it back to him, then Pathé, then, with Kerkorian by this time deep in his late eighties, Sony. The latter deal gave Kerkorian a profit of over $2 billion. He no doubt awaits doing it all over again. He is only ninety even now. There is plenty of time.

Five

UNDERSTAND THE MONEY

Business? It is quite simple.
It is other people's money. ·

Alexander Dumas fils

In a nutshell, that is exactly what it is. What the founding entrepreneur has to seek to do is to keep his or her own level of investment down, and other people's level of investment way up. But that does not mean giving away the farm. The entrepreneur should aim to own just as big a percentage of the company as he can, for as little personal financial exposure as can be got away with, and that is wholly possible if you have the skill and discipline to do it.

In the start-up's very early years, other people's money – third-party finance – will be next to impossible to recruit. Every penny will probably have to come from you, or from your family and your friends. In many ways, this is no bad thing. Were you to recruit a conventional venture capital investor at this stage, they would be investing at very low valuations indeed, and their terms would be extremely severe. On your own, you have a chance to develop value. You also have a chance to make absolutely sure that you fully comprehend your task. Frankly, either you are going to fail immediately, or you are going to become a real entrepreneur. You will have to demonstrate, to yourself, that you really know the basics of managing money. You have to generate customers, customers have to pay you and you are going to have to spend only what you have. It sounds simple, and so it is. It is not a bad thing to have the chance of polishing those arts on your own, at a moment when you are simply unable to fail.

If there is debt, it will have to be secured on a dependable asset from outside the company, most probably the family house. As the company moves forward, and starts generating profits and market position, the entrepreneur has something to sell. The brand has developed value (which has transmuted itself into price), and the attitude should be, and held with real determination, that if anyone wants to have a slice of that value, then they must pay the top dollar for it. If it is bank debt, then the bank should consider itself fortunate to have found such a comfortable home for its money, so the interest rate should be tight, the fees modest, and the pay-down programme thoroughly comfortable. Shop around, bank to bank, and get the best deal you can. If it is equity that you are selling – a share in the ownership – then your attitude should be that no one is going to be allowed to get in cheaply. That means that you must never go into negotiations too late, with your trousers around your ankles. If you have left it too late, anyone will be able to see that you have next to no cards to play. So do the deal in really good time (and this is where a discipline of regular forward cash-flow scheduling, done by yourself for yourself, really comes into play) and go for the very best price. By going for the best price you demonstrate a sense of real worth. Have the self-confidence – and negotiating technique – to make absolutely sure that happens. This will certainly turn out to be one of the few big plays of your life. Do not think of wasting it, for your family's sake.

The overriding goal is this: when the big financial wins occur, however many years later, it is you as the founding entrepreneur and the staff that have followed you that should proportionately benefit best of all. The financial backers, the providers of 'other people's money' whether they are providing debt or equity, should benefit fairly and respectably, but as comparatively modestly as it is possible for you to have pre-negotiated. Their objective will have been to squeeze you on the margin – that is to say to give you and your team a good enough deal on their entry into the company so that you are appropriately motivated for the future, but at the same time keep the cream for themselves. Your objective should be to squeeze *them* on the margin – to give them a good enough deal to get them in (you need them, otherwise you would not be talking to them) but have the cream on the cake left for you and the team.

That is your objective, and you must not lose sight of it, or miss a trick in achieving it. Do not be shy. That is what you and your team deserve, and you must be smart enough to achieve it. Remember why you started the business in the first place. It is always for the same reason. People start businesses because they yearn to start businesses. To express themselves, to realize an intuitive creative dream, to save themselves from committing the self-violation of spending the large part of their adult lives within the sterile embrace of big corporate life. Those are very good reasons. You and your family and your staff will have been through immense stress and effort in reaching where you now are. You have been through a huge change of life. You and your team have achieved great things. Make sure that it is you, and not the financial outsiders, particularly the venture capital players, who in time get the greatest slice of the financial win.

Redundancy is often the catalyst for the change of life we are talking about here; the change of life that first put you in a position to start the process of making your life mean something. If it is redundancy that you have been through, you will know that it can be both a bad and at the same time an exhilaratingly benevolent experience. Redundancy can prove for many people to have been a stunning, blinding act of mercy. Consider Silicon Valley, that iconic place of enterprise culture. Silicon Valley was born from the mass lay-offs in the US defence sector, the result of the ending of the Cold War. That sudden burst of homeless and available technological talent blended into an environment where US labour laws allowed a high degree of flexibility, the richest possible breeding ground for start-ups. In the UK technology sector a similar if less dramatic situation happened in the early 1980s when IBM and ICL were both laying off great swathes of employees. These people, both in California and the Thames Valley, became the IT entrepreneurs who rose to the fore some ten years later, peaking in the mid-to-late 1990s, every man jack of them by that point a dotcom legend, with equity and equity options giving them the aura of paper millionaires X times over. They were of course aided by the Dutch tulip bulb collective market madness of the time, but there it is. (And at a practical level they were more prosaically helped by changes in technology, notably the arrival of the low-cost PC, which in itself created a whole new sector of the software industry. But that is another story for another time.)

So there you have it. To create our new wave of business start-ups all we need is a short sharp recession with lots of job losses. Combine that with some sort of major technological change, mix it all in with government policies that provide significant tax advantages for entrepreneurs and investors, and then we will be getting somewhere!

Well – we *are* getting somewhere, though the collapse of the technology investment market has left a very nasty scar. The effect of that collapse was shown in the fact that immature British companies found it harder to secure financial backing in 2004 that at any time for a decade or more. The hangover from the dotcom boom continues to this day to haunt venture capitalists. That makes for dire straits, with industry sources suggesting that at any one time about 10 per cent of the 190,000 new businesses founded in the UK every year are in sore need of a cash injection. Only about 500 of these will be able to attract an equity investor of any description – which is quite a startling figure. Let's drill down into it a little further. In 2004 venture capitalists invested in just 286 early-stage companies in the UK – that is to say fledgling businesses that have yet to turn a profit and so find it very difficult to borrow from banks. That early-stage investment total was

15 per cent below the previous year, and one-third of the number at the time of the dotcom peak in 2000. The outcome of this was that the value of new UK investment fell from just over £5 billion in 2000 to barely £750 million in 2004. That is a huge fall. And the situation was worse in terms of venture capital investment into Europe, where industry reports show that the €30 billion invested in start-ups in the first two years of the new century has almost all been lost. That means that the 650 venture capital firms targeting fledgling companies in Europe have seen their funds nigh on destroyed, and they can only hope for recovery now by moving into much bigger deals in much more developed, mature companies.

But that is Europe; as far as Britain is concerned, for all the current malaise in investor attitudes it is difficult to conclude anything other than that these days there is truly a most firmly embedded enterprise culture. We now have over 200,000 more small businesses than we had ten years ago. On the latest figures available, the UK is showing the fastest growth rate in self-employment in living memory. Today the UK has almost 3.5 million self-employed people – in England alone 13 per cent of adults are now self-employed or wholly own a business, and a further 11 per cent, according to government research, are considering setting up a business too.

It really is quite a revolution, and yet the levels of entrepreneurial activity that are being reached in Britain – so very much ahead of the rest of Europe – are still lagging behind the US. The levels are also uneven. The average Scot, for example, is a lot less enterprising than his or her English counterpart. On recent figures the English start new businesses at an average rate of 42 per year per 10,000 adults, while the average rate north of the border is running at a comparatively paltry 28 per year. Why the difference? One reason is probably that the heavy industries such as coal, steel and shipbuilding, on which the Scottish economy relied for much of the nineteenth and twentieth centuries, are still much embedded within the Scottish culture, and are just not conducive to spawning the kind of companies that start small and grow big. Another explanation might be that because home ownership in Scotland is relatively low, fewer Scots have the collateral to raise the money needed to start new businesses. But the imbalance is nonetheless striking.

The UK overall will get there in all likelihood, however, and probably quite soon. The gap with the US really is closing, and closing fast, with the result that there has been a substantial creation of wealth and prosperity for individual communities throughout the land. The mood of the country is behind that. It likes what is happening. Both mature adults and young people are clearly positive about small businesses and entrepreneurs, to the extent that, according to government research, 93 per cent of adults admire people who run their own business and 64 per cent would encourage friends or relatives to start a business. And, in the same 2003 survey, no less than 43 per cent of students said they themselves wanted to start and run their own business some time in the future.

The Chancellor, Gordon Brown, has expressed the aim

that Britain should accelerate the number of entrepreneurial start-ups each year. He wants to improve the annual rate of business creation so that it is brought up to and even beyond the level of the US during his tenure of office. And to be fair to him, the Treasury under his leadership has gone a fair way towards assisting that, cutting audit, tax and VAT requirements on small firms. He has radically improved the tax regime for founding entrepreneurs, and importantly (and to some extent in defiance of Britain's traditional culture) has provided a sympathetic and swift recovery structure around personal insolvency. Brown has also created substantial incentives for investment in research and development, set up a new National Council for Graduate Entrepreneurs, and has established a new Enterprise Capital fund to finance small firms. His bold and imaginative 2002 Enterprise Act dealt with several important residual issues around competition and insolvency – the latter, as we have said, surprisingly sympathetic.

Gordon Brown clearly likes the word 'enterprise'. Politicians tend to – not least Mrs Thatcher, as we saw from the 'enterprise' zones she promoted when she first became prime minister of the country. French in origin, enterprise means, literally, a bold and arduous undertaking. You can say that again.

The Chancellor's goal is that Britain should have an extra two million businesses, or thereabouts, within five years. But what about the banks? It is the banks that at least partially hold the key to that level of acceleration, and without their intervention these goals can never be achieved. Well, they make appropriate noises, setting up units to help small businesses by means of professional advice and counselling. But the real need is not for advice and counselling. There is the feel of a Department of Trade and Industry outreach smudge around bank initiatives of that sort. The real need is not counselling, but access to debt at an affordable cost. One way of creating this is actually not in the banks' but in the Chancellor's hands. What we need above all else is an extension to the small business loan guarantee scheme.

As I write, businesses in the UK less than two years old can, under the scheme, get debt of up to £100,000, of which 75 per cent is guaranteed to the banks by means of government security. If the company has been trading for two years and more you can have up to £250,000 of debt with 85 per cent government protection, and with ten years to repay. But the bad news is very bad news. The founding entrepreneurs are means tested. Effectively, practically everyone therefore has to put up their house, although, as we have seen, that is pretty much par for the course in any situation. No – it is not the house that is the real problem, it is the fact that the debt, if you can get it, comes with a 2 per cent per annum surcharge, payable to the Department of Trade and Industry.

If ever I saw an asinine piece of misplaced dogma it is that – and it has been around too long. The whole purpose of the small business loan guarantee scheme – absolutely rightly – is to give start-up businesses with little personal asset collateral the best chance of surviving, then growing, and in time maturing into something really worthwhile. This surcharge fee – absolutely wrongly – makes survival considerably more difficult; indeed it can mean the difference between survival and failure, especially given that if you are to qualify for the scheme, you have to be small and vulnerable – no bigger than £5 million annual sales if you are a manufacturer, or a tiny £3 million if you are in the services industry.

I used a small business loan for the first two years or so of Waterstone's life. I scrapped it the moment I could, and for one reason only – that surcharge. All in all we had a slightly chequered history with that small business loan. When I was all set to go, with my £22,000 of equity and my business plan written, I decided to seek a financial partner. I realized it would probably prove almost impossible on a start-up, but I knew how far and fast I wanted to drive the business, and reckoned the earlier I had an institution on board the better.

The only realistic player for me was 3i (or ICFC as they were then called), and, eventually, after one meeting and a constant battery of hourly telephone calls from me, they agreed to subscribe the sum of £4,000 on the same terms as me (which I believe remains the smallest equity subscription 3i have ever made!). They did this simply to get me off the telephone, they told me later. Now I had £26,000, but I needed £100,000 to get the first store open (it is still there, in London's Old Brompton Road, and I cross myself when I pass it each morning . . .). I asked 3i to help me raise the £74,000 debt, explaining to them that I had tried but had not suc-ceeded in raising money on my house, as it had suddenly developed severe subsidence problems, and had to be completely underpinned. They told me that my only hope was a small business guarantee scheme loan. I asked them where to get that, and they suggested I called a young Barclay's manager at Cranleigh in Surrey, who they had heard was on the ball. I did so. He told me I could come down to Cranleigh. I made the most impassioned presentation of my plan, explaining that within ten years Waterstone's would be the biggest bookselling chain in the world outside the US. All we needed was a little help from him. Very interesting, he said, and asked if I had any more copies of the plan. I told him I didn't, but rushed off down Cranleigh high street, found a photocopy shop, and ran off fifteen more copies. I ran back to the bank and gave them to the manager. He flipped through them, and told me he would be in touch. He never was. I found out a little later what he had done with my lovely business plan. He had used it that very afternoon at a regional Barclay's seminar as an exhibit of the sort of company you should not lend money to under any circumstances . . .

I called 3i again, at least every hour like before. They sent me to a NatWest manager in Covent Garden. I again made the impassioned presentation, and when I had finished there was dead silence. He stared at me, and I stared at him. He shook his head. He told me that I was either a madman or a genius, he had no idea which, but did not much mind either way as he was retiring the following Tuesday. I could have the money.

Back to the 2 per cent surcharge. It should be scrapped

immediately; particularly so as its beneficiary, the laughingly incompetent and redundant DTI, provides absolutely nothing in return except for an ever-growing mountain of red tape and centralist business babble.

Putting aside the 2 per cent surcharge, and welcome as the Treasury's many new initiatives have been in recent years, there is room to go before the UK matches the less fiddly, simpler debt funding schemes that are available to founding entrepreneurs in the US. Most individual states have good schemes to offer. In New Hampshire, for example, founding entrepreneurs can readily qualify for as much as $1.5 million in state secured debt, of which as much as $500,000 can be allocated to working capital. The US Federal authorities also have many schemes, not least a $1 million debt line for small businesses of fewer than a hundred employees that are 51 per cent founding-owner controlled, and run by women or minorities (interest rates are negotiated between borrower and lender, but a Federal maximum is set). A surprisingly good euro facility is available too, in the European Investment Bank Loan Support Scheme. This programme provides for lower cost finance to support capital projects and fixed asset investment on projects costing £60,000 and over – firms eligible are those with fewer than 500 employees and less than £50 million in net fixed assets. The EIB provides the loan to support the development of projects that enrich infrastructure, trade, tourism and the environment within EU national borders.

So there is much to get at there. The 2 per cent loan surcharge aside, there have been some really good things coming from the Treasury in recent times that have a genuine sense of purpose in assisting founding entrepreneurs and their fledgling businesses to survive and prosper. Not least is the Alternative Investment Market (AIM) which has been a runaway success through the massive boost of the innovative tax breaks it now enjoys. You can get a company on to AIM just months after its birth, and some have done just that.

But more could be done of course – as is always the case. It would help, for instance, if the Chancellor instructed the Inland Revenue to desist from trying to call everyone employed, thus forcing them into the clutches of PAYE, and pushing them into the employer's national insurance contribution net. But to take one example of excellent recent legislative innovation, the availability of generous tax breaks for private individuals investing in unquoted companies has led to a proliferation of business angels. This, in a general sense, is undoubtedly seen as a most useful development. I have some doubts personally as to how it works in practice, as you will see in a moment, but the finance requirement in young UK companies of, say, £10,000 to £250,000 has proved in recent times to be very difficult indeed to satisfy, particularly so since 3i, in their previous incarnation as ICFC the granddaddy of them all (and historically the most prevalent provider of equity to young, small companies), has decided to turn its back on this sector and concentrate, as do almost all the other private equity groups, on the big players. That leaves a very big and worrying gap.

Business angels are wealthy entrepreneurial individuals who, encouraged by these new, increasingly generous tax breaks, personally provide equity for young companies, and then monitor most carefully what the start-up or early-stage company is doing with it. For sums above £250,000, angels invest predominantly through syndicates, of which these days there are plenty. Formal angel networking organizations advertise their presence through the Internet and the press and are a decidedly growing force. (Unsurprisingly so, when tax breaks for these angels include unlimited capital gains tax exemption at 40 per cent, inheritance tax exemption, and income tax relief at 20 per cent on investments up to £200,000.)

The Treasury has done an excellent job in attracting these people into small company investment, particularly when the company then receives, not through charity but through simple self-interest, good advice and mentoring by the angels, who are typically people who have retired from their own successful businesses. Far better this than the alternative of pitching for equity help from a Venture Capital Trust, every one of which has a predominantly tax-driven attitude to investment. The VCTs have proved to be very lowly per-formers, with a poor selection expertise. Consequently, their net asset values, across their industry, typically almost halved between their inception, in the mid 1990s, and their position seven or eight years later.

The Venture Capital Trusts have proved to be just too tax driven and thus commercially passive (and commercially under-informed) in style. What is more, they lack that added and very special cutting edge of motivation through direct personal investment. That is so important. Angels may only invest in two or three companies each. It is their own family money they are putting on the line, and they are looking not just at the tax breaks, but big wins too, for themselves and their families, in helping to nurse the management of their small investee companies through into a golden future. Particularly relevant is the point that as they are only going to be able to spread their money over two or three companies, then those companies are likely to be within a business sector of which the angel has personal experience and genuine expertise. That allows them to keep an eagle and expert eye on what is going on, particularly with regard to the quality of the management, observed day by day. They like their management to be hungry. If the angels lose their money, then they will want the management to lose everything.

This is the orthodox case for the business angel movement. I do not want to carp about this, as I know from my own acquaintance of several cases where the angel and his money have been of huge assistance to a fledgling entrepreneur. But I have to say I also know some other examples where it has been a personal disaster for the early-stage entrepreneur, who found the presence of a not entirely benevolent nor, as it proved, expert angel a very mixed blessing indeed. So I would say this: use an angel something of a penultimate resort. Penultimate, because you are not at the final moment where the angel's money is your only hope for the company's survival. Only bring an angel in if you are absolutely certain that the personal chemistry between you will work. Lay down absolutely clearly the limits of the angel's participation in the company's operational activities. And only bring an angel in at an entry price that you have negotiated with him, rather than one that he has forced on you – once again, that will be possible for you to do only if you have not allowed the situation to have drifted so far out of control that you have few negotiating cards left to play.

Maybe your young company can settle and grow just through cash-flow, and you can hold the business in your own hands for a time, without both outside debt and outside equity. That is absolutely the ideal, but unless you have really substantial personal funds to apply (Philip Green and Bhs!) this will be painfully slow progress, perhaps too slow to hold market position, retain momentum, and recruit decent staff. You could avoid the red tape of the small business guarantee scheme loans (and their pernicious 2 per cent DTI surcharge) and use less money, borrowing, as we have said, just against the security of your house, but you will really have to watch this so that you are not threatened, terminally, by a sudden rise in rates or an unexpected slump in the market – particularly if you are operating in a sector that is cyclical in nature.

Mark Derry, who has developed Loch Fyne Restaurants from scratch, has used private investment only, and has avoided approaching angels outside his acquaintance. I am rather admiring of his approach. Here is what he did. He went round to see over 200 friends and family and raised almost £1.5 million to get his business on the road. Apart from one or two bigger investments, most were just £5,000 or £6,000 a head. With this money in the bank and the first restaurants open, he later raised a further £4 million through two rounds of EIS funding (another government scheme that enables private investors to claim back the tax on money they invest in small businesses).

What Derry wanted to do was to make his mistakes in private. He wanted to keep full operational control in his own hands, make all his own decisions, and be the single focus of leadership for his staff. He opened restaurants, he closed restaurants (London was a disaster for him, where, such was the competitive pressure, he saw much lower sales and much higher costs) – everything he did was entirely up to him. What he signally did not want was someone sitting at his shoulder telling him, or 'advising' him, what to do. No angels, therefore. Just him. And he has done well, with the business growing within five years from nothing to twenty-nine provincial restaurants around the country, and an annual turnover of £30 million. Loch Fyne has now been acquired by a financial buyer for about £35 million, which is an excellent win for all those 200 family and friends who risked their money. It is just as well, of course, for the penalty of using family and friends in this way is that if the company had not succeeded, then the moral pressure on the founder would have been particularly onerous. What was wise of Derry was to cast the net so widely; individual stakes of £5,000 or so are relatively bearable if the company fails and the money is lost. With such small individual stakes he would also have probably been better placed to raise funds from his supporters individually once more, should an equity rights issue have been required for whatever reason.

Down the wire, had Mark Derry decided to hold the business for longer in order to build up its value further, a decent and sustained profit record would have given him access to long-term finance. But he would not have got the money for nothing. Asset finance is increasingly popular, and perhaps he would have looked at that. Invoice discounting too. Structured and integrated finance is applicable where funds are raised through a combination of methods – senior debt, mezzanine debt, loan stock and equity – good for cash-generative businesses with a low capital spend, as the emphasis is on long-term running yield. But long-term financial instruments – loans, asset-financed packages and commercial mortgages – are a difficult part of the financial jigsaw to slot into place. And a word of caution. One sees it too often. Many growing businesses fold because they fail to secure such finance, but an even greater number fold because their business, good as it is, has not been adequately primed to repay the long-term strategic debt that was put into place. Banks foreclose on you without a second thought. They very, very nearly did on Waterstone's in 1985. I remember that day vividly. We nearly lost the company. Cash-flow awareness and meticulous cash-flow planning is everything. I certainly learnt that lesson the hard way, and I suspect Mark Derry has too with Loch Fyne Restaurants.

I want now to move on to issues surrounding raising equity from the venture capital or private equity industry – when your company has reached a sufficient level of reliable profit generation you have a deal to offer them, and a negotiating hand to play. But before doing so I am going to linger for a moment on the vital importance of truly understanding cash-flow. It is not the finance director who needs to understand cash-flow, it is you. Finance directors will come and go, on occasion no doubt with your boot up their backsides, so it is you yourself that has to have a complete grasp of what is happening with your liquidity headroom, and what is likely to happen to it in the future. Prepare all your own forecasts. Look at the finance director's, and debate them in detail, but depend on your own. Calculate yourself, for yourself, as often as once every two weeks, monthly cash-flow projections for eighteen months rolling forward, starting each time you do it with a blank piece of paper. Be brutal with yourself in the understanding and acceptance of bad news. Never turn away from it. Play poker with others if you really have to, but never fool yourself. Always, personally, look the true situation directly in the eye.

As you concentrate your own focus so determinedly on cash-flow planning, you should be able to shield yourself from having the truth obfuscated by the bogs of accountant-speak and gobbledegook. The profession's procedures and priorities seem sometimes to have more in common with the pedantic, oblique mysteries of the Japanese tea ceremony than the crucial imperatives of keeping a company on the road. But the more you educate yourself to understand this whole financial area, the less likely you are to be fooled, or to miss a vital truth, and the better equipped you will be to negotiate with the providers of 'other people's money'.

Realize, for example, that traditional accounting, true to its origins as the guardian of assets and as the record-keeper of a corporation as a legal entity, furnishes data only on what has happened within the company as a possessor of static property. Traditional cost accounting, in contrast, has as its *raison d'être* its focus on improving profits by one means: minimizing your costs. So make yourself at least bullet-point-acquainted with the principles of not just that, but also what is called economic chain accounting, which provides detail of costs not just in your business but throughout your entire economic chain, from raw materials supplier to ultimate customer. General Motors invented economic chain accounting around the beginning of the twentieth century, on the realization of the essential truth that even then, at the height of its power, when it provided perhaps 70 per cent of all the parts and supplies that went into one of its finished cars, those costs incurred within GM itself accounted for less than one-tenth of what the customer was ultimately paying for that car. Sears Roebuck copied and modified this line of analysis in the 1920s, then Marks & Spencer and Toyota took it up after the Second World War. Finally our good friend and benefactor Sam Walton took it, adapted it for Wal-Mart, and changed the world.

Economic chain accounting was the foundation stone of Wal-Mart's early success. It still is. Watch to this day their buyers in China, and the techniques they employ in their tortuous negotiations with their suppliers. Every individual component of the cost structure in those products, prior to Wal-Mart agreeing to buy them, will have been broken down and examined and questioned. They would like to say they negotiate by logic, rather than brute force through buying power. We will pass on that perhaps. However, I was very struck by some comments I once read made by a partner of Accel Partners, the heavy-hitting Silicon Valley venture capital firm. Among their many successes, four or five years ago Accel formed Wal-Mart.com with Wal-Mart Stores. The thrust of what this practitioner was saying was that Accel always tried to remain very consistent in their analysis of any company in which they were looking to invest. Their focus, always, was very specifically on gross margins. Now – here is the interesting point. He said that nine out of ten chief executives they met were entirely unable to take Accel through a detailed analysis of their gross margin structure. But you have no choice when you are dealing with Wal-Mart. Conversations start and end with one thing. The gross margin structure. That is a night and day difference.

Wal-Mart is absolutely right. Economic chain accounting provides a very tight mindset in the hands of a player dedicated to its processes over an extended period of time. Wal-Mart is certainly that, though I have to say that there is something deeply depressing about the strip mall debasement of towns in the US. 'There are fewer and fewer somewheres in America, and more and more anywheres,' as John Updike put it, in his dismay. But Wal-Mart is there across the whole range of conservative, small-town America, and nothing will change that now. Prices are low, staff quality low, inventory unambitious if quite vast. But it is the prices that count. Wal-Mart's response to consumer pressure drives them lower and lower all the time. That pressure, based as we have said on its allegiance to the principles of economic chain accounting, governs everything that Wal-Mart does. 'It is too simplistic to say that we cut costs just by squeezing our suppliers,' said a Wal-Mart spokesman in January 2005. True. They also squeeze the store staff's remuneration just as far as they can do. Roger Blackwell, professor of marketing at Ohio State University, commented at that time, 'Wal-Mart is not really a customer of P&G or Gillette, they are a buying agent for the consumer – that does not change.' That is an interesting comment. You could say that being a buying agent for the consumer is a description of economic chain accounting in its purest form. Effectively the Wal-Mart stores are adjuncts to P&G and Gillette and other great brands – consumer warehouses one could say, umbilically tied to the storage warehouses. They all exchange consumer information the moment it becomes available. They are partners. And they all have the same need – efficiencies of scale to carry on matching the demands of consumers and their retail prices.

But the world never stands still. A newish technique, now fast establishing itself, is activity based accounting. This concentrates not on the minimizing of costs but on the maximizing of yields. You could say that it focuses on the creation of value, rather than on the avoidance of waste. Activity based accounting, and now its younger brothers such as EVA (economic value added), and what is referred to as the executive scoreboard, are all leading us in the same direction: the understanding that the enterprise is the creator of wealth and value rather than the possessor of static property. Or even, as in cost accounting, the steward of existing resources. And that is truly what businesses are, as I see them. An enterprise for the creation of wealth and value. That is why big corporations make asses of themselves when they study the newcomer's perilous balance sheets, and kill themselves laughing at them (remember WHSmith and Waterstone's); newcomers have the potential to leverage huge wealth creation from a tiny, fragile net asset base. Why? Because their brands have carried within them, from the very moment of their birth, that magic spark of creative genius which contains *value* instantaneously, and, in its own good time, *price*. That is their true 'goodwill', in my version of accounting-speak.

Right – we can now assume that you are going to take pains to educate yourself personally with a real understanding of finance, and, most importantly of all, its necessary disciplines around cash-flow planning. Cash-flow planning done for yourself, by yourself. You have to do this. You have a business that because of your personal creative genius and guts has shown it has staying power and real prospects, and you and your staff must ensure you achieve a high level of reward for that when the time comes. You have a dilemma, however. The company needs more money now to drive it forward, and the business has outrun its capacity to service more bank debt. You have run your eye over some alternatives – might there be more room in your working capital, for example, with the negotiation of longer credit days from your main suppliers? – but you have come to the conclusion that there is not too much there. The company needs more equity, therefore, and the problem is that you and your family have absolutely gone as far as you can go yourselves, and you have run out of friends to tap, even if you wanted to do so. Is it time, therefore, to take your chance with those gilded youths from the venture capital houses, and see if you can extract some decent equity investment money from them at a good price and with minimal and benign small print in the shareholders' agreement that will underlie the deal?

Before you do that, however, make sure you have a proper understanding as to what you are doing; how the private equity or venture capital industry works, how these people get their wins, and where and how they will be looking to impose on you, if they can, particularly advantageous terms for themselves. Incidentally, 'private equity' and 'venture capital' are effectively interchangeable terms, though the latter is perhaps more customarily used these days for investments into early-stage, immature companies, and the former for substantial equity transactions into established businesses.

So, who are we dealing with? Grasp the scale of the industry first of all. More than three million people in Britain – approximately 18 per cent of the entire work force outside the public sector – are employed in venture capital backed businesses, of an average turnover of about £70 million. In the last ten years the UK venture capital industry has invested over £30 billion in some 18,000 companies worldwide; of which £23 billion has been in the UK. Individually, the private equity firms have little or no public profile, yet their influence on the UK economy is vast – and growing. Some individuals have a strong City, if not public status – Sir Ronald Cohen at Apax, Guy Hands when at Nomura – and Jon Moulton, managing partner of Alchemy, achieved heavy press coverage both for himself and for the private equity world overall when bidding for Rover from BMW. That moment in 2000 marked something of a turning point in terms of public awareness of venture capitalists. Some observers were much in support of Moulton, and what he proposed for Rover. Others, however, portrayed him, and the venture capital world that he represented, as little more than a salivating vulture, there to strip assets down to the barest of bones before moving on to the next innocent victim.

Let us first make the case for the defence. You might call the KKRs, the 3is, Permiras and the Carlyle Groups the conglomerates of our age, the successors to Hanson, Trafalgar

House, Williams Industries and various others – but one big difference between venture capital backed businesses and the old conglomerates is that the former have shown a very much faster growth rate than the latter. An astonishing growth rate, in fact. A recent British Venture Capital Association report shows venture capital backed firms growing staff numbers at 24 per cent per annum. Compare that with only 2 or 3 per cent for national growth, and it is 70 per cent faster than companies within the FTSE 250. Look at the sales growth: in the four-year period to December 2004, private equity backed companies saw their annual sales rise by 40 per cent – double that of FTSE 100 companies. Investment rose by 34 per cent a year compared with a national increase of just 7 per cent.

The industry's supporters would say venture capitalists have a good record of getting behind a company and truly making it sing. A senior director who sat on the boards of both public companies and venture capital backed private ones would tell us that there is a particular glint in the eye of venture capital backed managers that makes them willing to work like mad in the pursuit of hitting the targets. Why? Because the individual managers have the opportunity for real personal capital growth. That does not and cannot exist in most public companies, with the exception of the incentive packages for the star-studded, tip-top leaders. In private equity held companies the chances of realizing really sub-stantial capital wins in a short timescale – either by equity or by bonuses – will typically extend right down to the middle management, and that makes a tremendous difference to the company's dynamism. The point is that it is a short timescale, just four or five years at the very most, and people can taste that win, early. They know it will come, because they know that the private equity managers have to have it, if they themselves (rather than their fund subscribers) are to make money. That dynamism comes too from the private equity players' mantra that it is better to have everyone overworked than to over-hire. When the staff in the business can see big capital wins for themselves just a little way down the track, then they would much rather overwork than see the company's profits slide down through the cost of excess head count.

The final point for the defence, perhaps, is this: when venture capitalists stick rigidly to their lasts (and, in my scar-tissued view, those extend not one millimetre beyond financial engineering, bank negotiations, accounting scrutiny, and the exploration of exit routes), they make extraordinarily effective shareholder partners in growing entrepreneurial companies. The best of them know that, and do so. They stick absolutely to their area of technical competence – superb technical competence, very often – and allow the managers, the experts in the business itself, to get on with it, albeit under as tight a financial framework as possible. The worst of them, however, do not – and I have worked personally with both sorts. The worst of them meddle and muddle with the business's operations, and disaffect the very management on whose expertise they depend to make them the money they aspire to. This sort pretends to have market expertise where they have none, insists on giving operational instructions, hires the wrong people into the company, talks nothing but money, and is impatient of the cultural aspirations of the company they have invested in – the hinterland of those companies, if you like, their identity upon which their long-term survival and prosperity will depend, long after the venture capitalists have slipped their cash into their bulging back pockets and departed the scene. (I think with a sympathetic shudder about, for example, a partnership an impresario of international fame had with a London venture-capital house. I talked to one of their partners at a party. Neither side, it would seem from what he told me, ever had the first idea what the other was on about. The venture capitalist talks about 'product'; the impresario talks about his artistes. The VC wants to turn a number of the impresario's theatres into – wait for it – casinos – for they calculate there is theatre 'oversupply' in venture capital-speak; the impresario wants to mount more new shows. The whole marriage sounded a total nightmare. I'm with the impresario. Totally.)

But – I repeat: the intellectual and technical quality of private equity house practitioners is generally very high. As long as they stick absolutely to their technical lasts (as above) then they can lead their investee companies into very rich pay days, and that is no small thing. But pay days are what we are talking about, and if you are going to negotiate a private equity house into your company, carry no illusions about that whatsoever. Be absolutely sure that that is really what you want. Could that pay day actually be premature?

Private equity remains resolutely misunderstood, its

defenders tend to say, but I wonder. Venture capital may have made great contributions to productivity and the Treasury, and its growth, as we have said, has been extraordinary, but for all its importance it is hardly a beacon for the general state of being of the UK economy, or anyone else's economy. There have been some genuine, staggering successes of course, and no one should carp at them: America's venture capitalists, in perhaps the best examples of all, did a magnificent job in developing Intel and Google from nothing more than bright ideas to corporations of gigantic worth. But these are rare exceptions. The industry's focus is very firmly on delivering returns to its investors – the subscribers to their funds, almost all of them institutions – and that within as short a time as possible. Perhaps it is not surprising, therefore, that senior private equity figures have underplayed the significance of that, particularly given the fact that their own personal rewards are so huge. The quicker the money goes back, the higher the percentage rate of return, and the higher the percentage rate of return, the bigger the fees for the venture capital practitioner (the deal is normally on the lines of a little less than a 2 per cent annual charge on the total funds raised, and then the managers are rewarded by a 20 per cent slice of whatever profits their investments make over, say, a 9 or 10 per cent per annum base line). So, as I say, the quicker the money goes back to the investors the better the managers fare. Exceeding a 10 per cent annual return becomes harder and harder the longer the money stays there unrealized.

It is a greedy world of very big personal wins. It is

probably not surprising, therefore, that even after twenty-five years the private equity model is still being assailed constantly by predictions of loss, scandal and disaster. The model certainly has many ingredients for trouble. Investments are typically so highly geared with bank loans and bonds that they can make a sound company become highly risky, should the market suddenly turn in the wrong direction. The details of deals are often too shrouded in fog and obfuscation. Financial relationships are complex and shifting. Internal incentives among the practitioners themselves are extremely, perhaps dangerously generous – and all of this is made even more dangerous with the investee businesses usually kept from the public gaze. The buy-out system, meanwhile, depends on practitioners being able to juggle the tasks of raising funds, the investment of funds already raised, the disposal of holdings and the return of successfully invested capital to backers. That may lead to poor exit decisions being made for companies that are by no means ready for realization, yet are forced into it because of the needs and timing of the private equity house's overall fund.

So how should you play these people? You really must not allow your fine company to be wasted now by a bad deal. My advice is this: first, try very hard not to put all your eggs in one basket. Ideally, split the deal between two, or even better, three different houses, so that you are not at the mercy of one. Make sure too that the houses you deal with have a good track record – not only for their wins, but for the way they deal with their companies' managers. Check them out by personal referencing. Secondly, never allow anyone else to undertake your negotiations for you. No agents. Use advisers for technical counselling only, and your lawyers as obfuscators if for any reason you are playing for time. Thirdly, go into negotiations with an absolutely clear picture of what your real goals are, then give not an inch in the contractual achievement of them. Ask for a somewhat better deal for yourself and your staff than you really need, then gradually scale back under negotiating pressure if needs be – provided you do not retreat any further than your base requirement. Also, be aware that the venture capitalists will try pretty well every time to improve radically the deal in their favour at the eleventh and final hour, reckoning that by this point you will give way simply to complete the transaction. Warn them in advance – and instruct your lawyers to tell their lawyers – that if they try that, you will definitely walk away, and offer the deal elsewhere (and be comforted that there are too many private equity houses around these days, with too much money, so all of them are in the market for a decent prospect). Look them in the eye and say that, and be quite clear that you mean it, as a point of honour, whatever the inconvenience to you might be. In this connection, try to negotiate as many of your advisers (lawyers, accountants) on to a success-only fee structure, so that if you do walk you are not stuck with onerous liabilities. Finally – and this is very difficult to achieve but you must do your darnedest – stick your heels in over the wording in the shareholders' agreement regarding realization. Try to ensure that the venture capitalists cannot proceed to sell the company behind your back prematurely. They will fight tooth and nail to be contractually able to do so. You must resist. Your goal here should be to ensure that the shareholders' agreement prevents them from conducting any realization talks with anyone without your knowledge and permission. Their fall back on this will be to provide a timescale – no talks without your permission and cooperation before, say, three years have passed. Try to make that four. You are unlikely to do much better than that.

If you are going to go down this route you are in for some tough talks, there are no two ways about it. But if you get what you wish to achieve, the venture capitalists' access to big money may be just what your company needs to bring it to its full market price under a short timescale. But – I repeat – be very careful over the exit provisions. Those are absolutely crucial. Be aware that unless restricted by contract the private equity managers will behave every time entirely within their own interests, rather than the founder's or the company's. If they need to dump the company prematurely they will do so, quite shamelessly.

Sometimes it really is difficult to take the private equity players' integrity seriously. It is true that selling down positions to cover start-up costs happens to be business strategy, but I do not think it is unfair to argue that the epoch-making dotcom collapse, for example, was caused in part by them. They were just too quick and too eager to get their money out, and ruined whatever chances the better dotcoms had of stabilizing their positions, and their shareholders overall of minimizing their losses. *Bloomberg Markets* magazine gave us a pointed example of this:

> The conflict of interest between venture capitalists and the public is well illustrated by the case of MyPoints.com in 2000, a US Internet direct marketing firm. That was quite a seminal year for the dotcoms. With just four months' cash left, MyPoints filed to raise almost $200 million by selling as many as four million shares to the public. At first blush, the offering would have appeared to refill MyPoints' coffers in exactly the way the company desperately needed. A closer look revealed that 40 per cent of the shares on offer were actually being sold by venture capital insiders. Thus almost half the money seemingly destined for the company, and only just in time for its survival, got diverted to insiders.

Another notable insider sell-off occurred at about the same time, again in the US, at the Internet real estate agent Home-Store.com. They were in a better position than MyPoints in that they were not leaving matters so late, and had enough cash remaining to last a little over a year. The stock came public at $20, rose to a high of $138, then slipped to $50. Five months later HomeStore announced a $900 million secondary offering, in which the venture capital insider shareholders reaped more than half the proceeds.

The gilded ones are a tough play. The rules they play by are selfish and single-minded. But, as I have said, their core competencies are often of an extraordinarily high standard, and this can have real benefits for you. You will find, for example, that if you have a good venture capital house on board your company will almost certainly find itself treated with increased respect by the banks. And increased respect from the banks means improved access to competitively priced debt. Banks know that the financial modelling skills of the private equity practitioners are of a standard all their own – and that gives them much comfort. It is largely because of the banks' enthusiasm for the private equity industry that the total value of venture capital activities has grown so considerably in recent years. Their game is always the same, and it suits the banks very well indeed: select a fragmented industry that provides companies with a strong cash-flow and an ability to pay down debt quickly; then work with a respected and hungry management team and set them to work. Industries that throw off cash such as support services, computers and health care are particularly attractive. It is comparatively easy to squeeze extra stated profits out of a business by cutting capital investment, scrimping on service and letting the pension-fund deficit rack up. In this way, private equity backed companies are adept at polishing up businesses over three years or so for resale. Creating sustainable long-term value is, of course, a much harder proposition. That is not what the venture capitalists do. Nor, in fairness, is it what they claim to do.

There are far more people looking to move into private equity firms than there is space available, such is the much publicized personal wealth of some of the stars of the field. It is difficult to pin down the exact numbers around the profits made by venture capital investment staff, as those are derived from the return of their investment fund as a whole, rather than on a deal-by-deal basis. For example, Stephen Grabiner, former business head of the *Daily Telegraph*, and now head of Apax Partners' media team, will have netted millions from the sale of Yell, British Telecom's former yellow pages business. Apax as a firm made a gain for their funds of at least £360 million – but Grabiner's precise personal win will depend on how well the other companies within Apax's media investments fare.

But it is two-way traffic. Increasingly, star performers are leaving public companies to join private equity backed ventures. Stephen Sunnucks goes from CEO of New Look to the private equity backed buy-out of Phase Eight. Jack Welch, no less, the legendary former leader of General Electric, is now at Clayton, Dubilier & Rice. Lou Gerstner leaves IBM and becomes chairman of Carlyle. Lord Hollick goes from United Business Media to KKR, saying that in becoming a private equity principal he will be able to 'focus on running businesses rather than on shareholder relations and corporate governance'. As chief executive at UBM he might easily have spent perhaps one-fifth of his time dealing with shareholders. Now he will be able to continue doing deals, with access to almost bottomless finances. He will be able to share in the spoils, and he will be free of all the tedious demands of corporate governance that now dictate the behaviour of quoted companies. The flood of talent into private equity spells out that it is not only the money that appeals, but the freedom.

Every day one reads of managers becoming venture capital principals, and managers moving over to run venture capital buy-outs. The latter is hardly surprising, given the size of the potential windfalls. The truth is that for most people the chance of making a multimillion pound win will only be found by being a participating manager in a leveraged buy-out. Typically, a small group of senior managers will be virtually gifted a 20 per cent or even 25 per cent share of the business. Three or four years later, when the company is exited once more, those managers can find that they have made for themselves and their families capital windfalls of £10 million a head, and more. Tragus – Bella Italia and Café Rouge – is a stunning example of this. The management team made a complete killing. ECI paid Whitbread £11 million in 2002 and not much more than two years later sold the company on to Legal & General Ventures for £107 million. Whitbread were insane to sell off the two brands at the price they did, if not necessarily wrong to slim down their over-large operating portfolio. But the price they sold at was a total insanity, however one looks at it. Unfairly no doubt, but it makes one just a little bit uncomfortable that Sir John Banham, a recent Whitbread chairman, was, as chairman of ECI, the buyer.

These days such windfalls – perhaps the equivalent remuneration of what the managers would otherwise have earned in total over the course of an entire forty-year career – in the UK come heavily sheltered from tax of more than 10 per cent. They are life-changing wins in prospect. Yes, it will in all likelihood have been intensely stressful. Meddled with or not, the meetings with the debt providers and the venture capitalists will be extremely demanding, and, if trading drifts away from the leveraged buy-out model, often painfully accusatory. But one great benefit is that the managers can move quickly to change something by getting all the decision makers in one room, and then doing it. Another is that the company can embark on the necessary longer-term restructuring which will damage your profits in the short term, but bring home real wins two or three years down the line.

So, if you are going to talk to venture capital houses, for goodness' sake know what you are doing. The best of them may prove to be fine partners, as long as you understand, and respect, that they will wish to exit themselves within four years at the latest. The worst of them will be an arrogant nightmare. In all circumstances, try, with your lawyer's assistance, to ensure that as much of your perception of the operating needs of the company for those four years is encompassed and articulated within the shareholders' agree-ment. Make sure, vitally, that the capital expenditure you wish to undertake over that programme is properly enshrined in there. Staffing levels too. Reduce to the minimum, right up front, those matters of detail that can be a source of quar-relling later on. Down the line you will be glad that you did.

But the real issue here is over the exiting. If you do not want your company to go to a liquidity event within the venture capitalists' short timetable, then do not do a deal with them. Have one more look around to see if there is another, more appropriate partner for you. The best of all are the true private equity houses, the traditional funders: the investment arms of family-owned major businesses, usually, who might be prepared to come alongside you as a true partner, quietly letting the company develop along on its way at a steady, reliable pace, until eventually, perhaps six or seven years, even a decade later, it becomes a really major player. These true private equity providers are very hard to find, but the families do exist, in Britain, in Europe, in North America, throughout the developed world. One could say that the Rockefellers and the Whitneys started it all. If you have an entrée to these people, use it, and explore what might be done. They are by far the best sources of equity support, if you can find it.

So – pause, research and think. Truly identify and work through your options. Make sure that what you do is absolutely right for you and the staff and the company. For 'other people's money' does not come free. There is a price to pay for everything.

Six

VALUE MATTERS – PRICE DOESN'T

Try not to become a man of success, but rather try to become a man of value.

Albert Einstein

One of the pleasures of operating within the private sector is that one is gloriously free from the great lie which sits over the ownership structure of all big public corporations, and one which, from my youngest working days, has always annoyed me in its moral dishonesty. Here is the lie: the concept that public corporation shareholders are the 'owners' of those businesses. The truth is that the vast majority of corporate shareholders have never invested one single penny into their investee companies in their lives. They hold their shares on a wholly different basis, simply trading them day by day with other traders.

There is nothing wrong with that, any more than there is anything wrong with a punter having a bet on a horse, but the punter does not then pretend he owns the horse, and is therefore responsible for its health and welfare. '*Your* company had a strong/rather less than strong year . . .' drivels the public company chairman in the annual report. He is addressing himself of course to those who happen, much by chance, to be on the share register just at the snapshot moment. *Your* company indeed. Just because some hedge fund speculator has been shorting on Unilever, and is buying in shares to close his position overnight, does not make him in any ethical, moral sense an *owner* of Unilever for the hours those shares are held. Unilever is owned by those who have a real, honourable stake in it: its staff past and present most importantly of all. They, as much as anyone, own Unilever, because Unilever is a living, organic body. One could say perhaps that Unilever actually owns itself. Unilever has value in its being. Hedge funds deal not in value but in price. Value and price are different concepts. Supporting a loyal employee through a nervous breakdown and nursing that person back to self-esteem, and work, is an action and a concept of value. It has nothing to do with price. Arbitraging Unilever shares and making a quick turn on a momentary differential between the Dutch and London stock markets is a thing of price. It has nothing to do with value.

As Charles Handy has said:

> the assumption throughout the traditional Anglo-American model of capitalism (it is not quite the same in Europe, Japan or China) is that the public company is a piece of property, owned by the people who have bought shares in it. They own it, therefore they can sell it, if they so decide – not just their own shares, but the piece of property, the entire company. Is that property at all? An advertising agency, a design house, a software company, a newspaper group – their tangible, fixed assets (financed in part by those shareholders who actually subscribed in the company rather than bought their shares on the secondary market) will in all likelihood be worth very considerably less than the market

value of the company. What's the difference between the two? People, that is the difference. The aggregate flair and wisdom and market nous of the people working there.

The City, or Wall Street, owns the assets, yes, and if the company goes into liquidation, whatever those assets sell for goes to them. But they also think they own the rest of it – the often colossal differential between the break-up value of the financial assets and what the company is worth in the market (the so-called 'goodwill'). Well, do they? That goodwill is actually people. People's interpretation of the company's embedded culture, and where they could take that. You cannot own people. They die. They decide to join a competitor. They leave. You do not, and, thank God, cannot, own people at all.

The stock market – the secondary market where people simply buy and sell shares between themselves, with no money going to the company, and which is simply a mechanism for gambling – could be argued to have no real right to sell companies over the heads of those that work there. A public company's share price does not automatically reflect the 'value' of that or any business. The stock market is just that – merely a market. And, as Yale economist Robert Shiller has said, like all markets the stock market is a thing of hope, frustration, greed and fear.

No – the moral truth is that the company is actually 'owned' by its staff, and by those investors who have truly invested – that is to say subscribed their investment money –

in the company itself. Everyone else is a gambler. The money from the secondary market – most of the London Stock Exchange and most of Wall Street – goes nowhere near the company.

Now, here is the rub. I believe it should, and in this way. There should be a royalty paid to the company of X per cent and Y per cent on the value of each transaction made – X per cent from the seller and Y per cent from the buyer. By these means the company being betted on – that is the real 'owners' of the company, the staff, the pensioners, the genuine, primary investors – will benefit. They will enjoy a new revenue stream that will boost their coffers and enable them to invest and reinvest into the company's development.

Now that really would be a revolution – and what an effective one! I would really like to see that happen. The true owners, the true investors, become beneficiaries of secondary trades. Let everyone gamble as much as they want. The more they do so, the more cashflows into the company, and the better that is for the staff, the pensioners, the customers, the suppliers, and indeed the founding, direct subscribing, non-buying and -selling shareholders. Maybe we should go the whole hog, as Charles Handy has suggested, and give all the staff and the direct subscribing shareholders A shares – voting shares – and all the gamblers B shares – non-voting shares. But maybe that is a step too far. For me, cash royalties on the gamblers' transactions would be fair and morally right.

I abhor pretence, and the present system is just that – pretence. '*Your* company' indeed! Public companies do not really use the stock market to raise money; they raise money from the banks, and by retaining earnings. They use it simply to put a market price on the company's value to enable staff and founders to get liquidity into the personal wealth they have built in their stakes. There is nothing wrong in that of course. But the act of doing it transmutes the company into a mechanism for gambling. Not investment – gambling. And the fact of that should be far more transparently presented.

So, in that and in several other ways corporate capitalism no longer feels quite right. One could say that capitalism has been a reasonable system, but is now in an unreasonable condition, and that is primarily because the concept of corporate ownership, and the responsibility that brings to owners, has been coarsened and weakened. There will be so much change moving forward now, so much flux. Some of that change will be benevolent and some destructive. Big corporations have been around since the latter years of the nineteenth century but for how much longer? As legal entities they will survive, no doubt, but in few other ways that we would recognize. Actually, that is probably something to look forward to. Some would go so far as to say that Western capitalism is beginning to feel tired, sordid and degenerate, parodied for us in a ghastly, pantomime form, by the current crop of Russian oligarchs. But here in the West too. In the US Dennis Kozlowski, former chief executive of Tyco, the electronic-component maker, goes off to jail in handcuffs for what could be twenty-five years in a state prison for stealing hundreds of millions of pounds from the company. Unlike Enron and

WorldCom, Tyco survived the scandal. We in Britain have similar tales to tell, with the Rover story ever fresh in our minds. On both sides of the Atlantic, there is a growing trend of evidence that the ugliest aspects of corporate capitalism are beginning to show through. Personal greed, untouched by principle and ethics, is too emphatically dominant.

Take the trend of gross overpayment of corporate executives. Top business leaders have become like sports heroes without the talent. You need not have any real knowledge of the business you are getting into, or any real knowledge of business of any sort, as was claimed in his defence proceedings by Bernie Ebbers, the former WorldCom CEO convicted on securities fraud and conspiracy charges and for filing false documents with regulators. American executives have reached sky-high compensation levels. Why? They make money for shareholders. If they did not, then the capitalists would not give it to them. And yet, and yet . . . *Barron's* reports that over the last ten years the compensation of top executives in America grew at twice the rate of corporate profits. Read that again. *Twice* the rate. In the period 1993 to 1995, the top five officers of public companies were paid just under 5 per cent of corporate profits. From 2001 to 2003, the level jumped to 10 per cent. In the decade ending 2003, these executives took $290 billion. Pearl Meyer & Partners looked at nearly 200 of the largest companies in the US. They found the average CEO made $10 million in 2004 – up more than 12 per cent from the year before. Bill Bonner's *The Daily Reckoning* points out that Carly Fiorina got more than $40 million from

Hewlett-Packard. Scott Livengood gets $46,000 per month consulting for Krispy Kreme, the company he personally glazed with losses. Franklin Raines got booted out of Fannie Mae but still gets $114,000 per month in pension benefits. GM's Rick Wagoner got a pay hike, to over $2 million, having guided the company to its biggest loss in a decade. Executive bonuses at one hundred big US companies rose by more than 46 per cent in 2004, to an average of more than $1 million, according to a study by Mercer Human Resource Consulting cited in the *Washington Post*. Or consider another study, undertaken by professors at Harvard and Cornell, that found executive pay at companies in the Standard & Poor's 500 Index almost tripled in a decade to an average of over $10 million in 2002.

Why pay these people so much? Would they be less motivated with $8 million, Bill Bonner asks? Would they be able to quit their night job if they earned only $5 million? Would companies be unable to find qualified candidates if they offered only $3 million? But then, you may worry, what if the company does not do well? Again, recent history shows us that you can fail miserably and still make a lot of money. See above – Scott Livengood and Rick Wagoner. Or have a look at Sir Peter Davis's recent exit package from the imploding Sainsbury's.

Another thing: next time you hear a chief executive go on about teamwork, about how 'we' did it by all pulling together, ask who is getting what kind of bonus. When you hear that chief executive boasting about taking the long view, ask how those bonuses are calculated. If cooperation and foresight are so important, why have these few been cashing in on generous stock options? Do we take the money back when the price plummets? Is it not time to recognize this kind of executive compensation for what it is: a form of corruption, not only of our institutions, but of our societies as democratic systems?

So once more – why should all this be? Why would capitalists allow their paid employees such a large and mushrooming share of what is actually owned by them? Could competent people not be found for less? On the one hand there is no answer. Many of the overpaid employees have proved themselves to be incompetents on any scale. But on the other hand there *is* an answer. Capitalism in its original, purist form has disappeared from big corporate life. There are no owners (bar, in the purest sense, the staff) of these huge public companies. Ownership carries a real burden of moral responsibility. These shareholders are not owners in this, the only true sense, at all. They are speculators. They are gamblers, in one minute and out the next. There is nothing inherently wrong with that, but it lies against any possibility of there being any sense of 'ownership' carrying moral and corporate responsibility.

So what is being illustrated here is the age-old, inescapable rule, that over time, every institution man ever creates – even one as nimble and adroit as capitalism – has a way of degenerating and corrupting itself. Everything, eventually, inevitably, falls apart. New institutions form themselves, but the old decay and die. As Bill Bounce says, the Catholic Church under the Medici popes would have been barely recognizable to St Peter. American consumption-led materialism today would have been repulsive to the nation's founding fathers. And capitalism in 2005 is a far different thing from the capitalism – benign, altruistic, socially idealistic – of Andrew Carnegie or John D. Rockefeller.

Everything ends. At the moment there is a sense of unease and urgency. Too many things are straying uncomfortably far from familiar landmarks. But maybe those landmarks were more short term than we had thought. Throughout the broad sweep of human history a worker in China earned much the same as a worker in Europe. The industrial revolution threw that savagely out of balance, but now, slowly, we are returning to the mean, as wages begin to rise in the East. It will be two or three generations at least before we are back in balance, but it will happen. For now we have the absurdity of Asians making things and selling them to the Americans in such volumes that the only way the Americans can pay for them is to provide the Asians with IOUs, which they can then either sit on, or use to buy up American productive capacity. The Americans are currently providing the world with the biggest vendor financing of all time. It is insane. And it is put into context by the fact that the fastest-growing categories in US employment are administration, health care, construction and real estate, and restaurants. In other words, many of the new jobs created involve building houses for people and serving them dinner. Nearly all of them are related to consumption – and practically none of them help ease America's trade deficit.

No – capitalism is not right in its current form, and the mood of the people is for change, and change will come. 'The mood of the people' – Hegel's 'zeitgeist' – is always an interesting concept: the way a single overriding sentiment infects and identifies one generation in comparison with the next.

That is the current state of capitalism for you, and I do not like it. I also dislike the received wisdom that the totally deregulated market place, the parody of the Anglo-Saxon model, is the only way forward. It is not. It is true that the French model, burdened by top-heavy bureaucracy, allied with the moral coarsening of an accelerating black economy ripping off the social benefits system, does not work now and will not in the future. The Swedish model, though, little considered these days by the rest of the world, most certainly does. We are proud of our current growth rates and unemployment levels, but in Sweden they are at least as good. The Swedish budget is in healthy surplus and has been so for some time – in sharp contrast to Britain, and emphatically more so to the United States – yet no other nation has developed their welfare state to the same extent. Swedish working conditions and the safety net protections for their workforce can hardly be matched anywhere else in the world, nor their equitable income distribution, underlined by the Swedes' distaste for vulgarly overpriced executive remuneration. Their life expectancy is the highest anywhere, and state pensions generous. The workforce is highly educated and gives high productivity, which is why major corporations such as Volvo and Ericsson stay there. And, as evidence from studies conducted by the London School of Economics have demonstrated, it is Sweden's high-tax model that actually enables the poor to achieve social mobility, rather than the superficially meritocratic, low-tax American one. So, the Swedes have achieved a very great deal. Theirs is a society of 'value'. Our Anglo-Saxon model does not have a monopoly on value.

I appreciate that quite a lot of this book has talked, perhaps portentously, about terms and concepts such as 'honour' and 'value'. Honour and value come in many forms of course, and it may be odd in some eyes that I, in writing a book about the entrepreneurial life, am so admiring of a society such as Sweden's. Sweden is a society of value, but not necessarily entrepreneurial values. I do not believe there is a contradiction, however. What I like in life is comradeship, and team loyalty, and courage, and a sense of common purpose towards the achievement of a worthwhile and honourable goal. And a sense of being true to oneself, by means of a compulsion to work one's socks off in a cause or a venture in which one wholly believes. A commitment to life, really. As Emile Zola wrote in *Le Docteur Pascal*, 'The only basis for living is believing in life, loving it, and applying the whole force of one's intellect to know it better.' That is the main reason why I am drawn to the entrepreneurial life myself, and why I am attracted to the company of other entrepreneurs.

Even in those years when I was struggling along in conventional corporate life I knew it to be so. The moment I threw over the old life and went off to try my hand at freedom, I immediately felt comfortable in my own skin. I had never had that feeling before. I had been pretending to be X and Y – but none of it was me. I had no commitment – or, more accurately, no cause to attach commitment to. I felt the most overwhelming need to make my personal mark on the world, to fight my own fights, to win my own wars. I had no fear whatsoever of failure or the consequences of that – though I should have done of course, in practical terms, with children to support. Quite simply, by doing this, I found happiness. And pride.

That is why I have written this book, because I would like to do what I can to encourage others like me to experience the same. The world is changing so fast. Capitalism as we have known it is not going to survive – though it will evolve, one has to believe and trust, into something healthier and more relevant to people's need for purpose and self-improvement. Besides, and this is a point that I really want to stress, capitalism, in the conventional sense, is not really the world that entrepreneurs, in their souls and minds, actually inhabit. Their world is that of teams winning the fight together, acting as catalysts for change and innovation, supporting one another in great adventures and initiatives. I do not care if there are Adam Smith motives of self-interest in that or not. Why should there not be? I realize that the teachings of Jeremy Bentham, James Mill and Adam Smith led us in time, as the message coarsened, to the Poor Law of 1834, that particularly savage piece of Victorian legislation attacked by Dickens in *Oliver Twist* (I admire the way that Dickens always maintained his belief in the power of benevolence). But self-interest is the way the world works, and on the whole it works happily, and in a subtle manner. It is not the great riches of capitalism that right-minded people seek above all else. It is personal and team achievement. It is happiness. It is lives well spent, as Andrew Carnegie's was. At the end of the day, it is moral quality. It is a sense of purpose. A sense of worth and continuity and pattern.

Steve Jobs, CEO of Apple Computer and Pixar Animation Studios, calls it 'connecting the dots'. His is an extraordinary story, and it is that of a genius of an entrepreneur. Steve Jobs's biological mother was a young, unmarried college graduate who decided to put her child up for adoption by a family of similar educational background. There was a muddle at the adoption agency, however, and he was actually taken in by a working class family of no education whatsoever. They were good people, though, and gave their word that the baby would be given a college education when the time came. They stuck to their word, and at seventeen Jobs went to the university of his choice: Reed College in Oregon. Beginning to realize, however, that the tuition fees were burning up his parents' entire life savings, and consequently full of remorse, he dropped out of college after just six months. He stayed, though, on the college's fringes, sneaking into lectures, sleeping in friends' rooms, returning

Coca-Cola bottles for the five-cent deposits, walking seven miles across town each Sunday night for the free meal at the Hare Krishna temple. Looking back at this period in later life – in hindsight 'connecting the dots' – he saw that it had offered him a priceless experience. For example, Reed College prided itself on being at the cutting edge of calligraphy – by tradition, throughout the campus each poster, each label, each notice was painstakingly and beautifully hand calligraphed. Fascinated, Jobs then learnt about serif and sans serif typefaces, about varying the amount of space between different letter combinations – all the little techniques and tricks of the trade that make aesthetically lovely typography what it is. He was not to know it at the time, but all this came precisely into context a few years later, when he and his colleagues were designing the first Macintosh computer – the first computer with beautiful typography, later copied by Windows. If Jobs had never dropped out from his course, he would never have dropped in to the calligraphy classes, and none of this would ever have happened.

You cannot connect the dots when the dots of your life are happening to you, because you cannot, without foresight, see their pattern. In later years, with hindsight, their pattern and their thread become absolutely clear. Take the next stage of Steve Jobs's quite marvellous life. He started Apple in his parents' garage at the age of twenty. Ten years later the Macintosh was launched, and Apple was a $2 billion public company with over 4,000 employees. But Jobs and his main executive partner, recently recruited, fell out with each other, and his board turned against him. Jobs was fired from the company he had created amid considerable public exposure. He felt shamed, and humiliated, and at the point of running away.

He did not see it then (one never does) but getting fired from his creation, and all the pain he incurred because of that, turned out to be the best thing that ever happened to him. 'The heaviness of being successful,' he puts it now, 'was replaced by the lightness of being a beginner again, less sure about everything. It freed me to enter one of the most creative periods of my life.' Creative it certainly was. During the next five years he started a company called NeXT, and then Pixar, which, brilliantly, went on to create the world's first computer-animated feature film – *Toy Story*, no less. Pixar is now the most successful animation studio in the world. And in a bizarre twist of events Apple bought NeXT and Jobs returned to Apple, where the innovative NeXT technology is the prime driver behind Apple's current renaissance.

But the dots go on connecting, and – as happens to all of us – the thread of Jobs's life winds on, as hindsight shows. His life imploded once more, horrifyingly and recently, when he learnt that he had advanced pancreatic cancer. Normally almost immediately fatal, it transpired that he had contracted a rare form of the disease that is operable, and he has survived. But the brush with mortality has reminded him of what he already knew and preached, that each day should be lived not so much as if it was your last, but in the realization that almost everything – all expectations, all pride, all fear of embarrassment or failure – fall away in the face of death. 'Remembering that you are going to die is the best way I know to avoid the trap of thinking that you have something to lose,' he told 5,000 Stanford University graduates in a wonderfully inspirational recent commencement address:

No one wants to die. But no one has ever escaped it. And that is as it should be, because Death is very likely the single best invention of Life. It is Life's change agent. It clears out the old to make way for the new. Right now the new is you, but someday not too long from now you will gradually become the old and be cleared away.

I wasted too much of my own life living in someone else's skin. A lot of us do, and it burns up our days. Our time on earth is so short. We have to swim on our own, and for ourselves. We must never be trapped by dogma – which is living within the confines of other people's thinking, and just as likely to be flawed as true. We will be swimming against the stream, and determined to do so. 'Never let the noise of other people's opinions drown out your own inner voice,' says Jobs. 'And – most important – have the courage to follow your heart and intuition. They somehow already know what you truly want to become.'

So there we have it – listen to what your heart is telling you. Trust in your personal intuition. And your hinterland, of course, and the certainty that no life is worth living without a true roundness of spirit. There is a simple Apache blessing that I very much like. I first heard it many years ago, and it has always stuck with me. So, I start the book with Kipling, and I close the book with this. To me, it is not such a leap.

'May you walk gently through the world and know its beauty, all the days of your life.'

Bibliography

Bentham, Jeremy *The Works of Jeremy Bentham*, 2 vols
(London, 1838–43, reprinted New York, 1962).

Covey, Stephen R. *The Seven Habits of Highly Effective People:
Restoring the Character Ethic* (New York, 1989).

Christensen, Clayton *Seeing What's Next?: Using the Theories of
Innovation to Predict Industry Change* (Boston, 2004).

Drucker, Peter *Concept of the Corporation* (New York, 1946).

—— *The Practice of Management* (New York, 1954).

—— *Innovation and Entrepreneurship* (New York, 1985).

—— *The Essential Drucker* (New York, 2001).

Ghoshal, Sumantra *The Individualized Corporation* (New York,
1997).

—— 'Beware the Busy Manager', *Harvard Business Review*
(1 February 2002).

Handy, Charles *The Empty Raincoat: Making Sense of the
Future* (London, 1994).

—— *Beyond Certainty: The Changing Worlds of
Organisations* (Boston, 1996).

—— *The Hungry Spirit: Beyond Capitalism* (London, 1997).

—— *The New Alchemists: How Visionary People Make
Something Out of Nothing* (London, 1999).

—— *The Elephant and the Flea: Reflections of a Reluctant
Capitalist* (London, 2002).

Jung, Carl *The Essential Jung* (Princeton, 1983).

Krugman, Paul R. *The Age of Diminished Expectations* (Boston, 1997).

Mintzberg, Henry 'Planning on the Left Side and Managing on the Right', *Harvard Business Review* (1 July 1976).

—— 'The Rise and Fall of Strategic Planning', *Harvard Business Review* (1 January 1994).

—— 'Musings on Management', *Harvard Business Review* (1 July 1996).

Ohmae, Kenichi *The Invisible Continent: Four Strategic Imperatives of the New Economy* (New York, 2000).

Peppers, Don *Enterprise One to One* (New York, 1997).

Peters, Tom *A Passion for Excellence* (New York, 1986).

—— *Thriving on Chaos* (New York, 1987).

—— *Sound Management* (New York, 1990).

—— *Fragile People* (New York, 1991).

—— *Liberation Management* (New York, 1992).

—— *The Pursuit of Wow!* (New York, 1994).

—— *The Circle of Innovation* (New York, 1997).

—— *The New Bottom Line* (New York, 1997).

—— *Reinventing Work* (New York, 2000).

—— *Re-Imagine!* (New York, 2003).

Porter, Michael *Competitive Strategy* (New York, 1980).

—— *Cases in Competitive Strategy* (New York, 1982).

—— 'From Competitive Advantage to Corporate Strategy', *Harvard Business Review* (1 May 1987).

—— 'What is Strategy?', *Harvard Business Review* (1 November 1996).

Shiller, Robert *Irrational Exuberance* (Princeton, 2000).

Smiles, Samuel *Self-Help* (London, 1859).

Smith, Adam *The Wealth of Nations* (London, 1776).

Index

INDEX